THE BOOK OF
Kink

THE BOOK OF
Kink

Sex Beyond the Missionary

EVA CHRISTINA

A PERIGEE BOOK

A PERIGEE BOOK
Published by the Penguin Group
Penguin Group (USA) Inc.
375 Hudson Street, New York, New York 10014, USA
Penguin Group (Canada), 90 Eglinton Avenue East, Suite 700, Toronto, Ontario M4P 2Y3, Canada
(a division of Pearson Penguin Canada Inc.)
Penguin Books Ltd., 80 Strand, London WC2R 0RL, England
Penguin Group Ireland, 25 St. Stephen's Green, Dublin 2, Ireland (a division of Penguin Books Ltd.)
Penguin Group (Australia), 250 Camberwell Road, Camberwell, Victoria 3124, Australia
(a division of Pearson Australia Group Pty. Ltd.)
Penguin Books India Pvt. Ltd., 11 Community Centre, Panchsheel Park, New Delhi—110 017, India
Penguin Group (NZ), 67 Apollo Drive, Rosedale, Auckland 0632, New Zealand
(a division of Pearson New Zealand Ltd.)
Penguin Books (South Africa) (Pty.) Ltd., 24 Sturdee Avenue, Rosebank, Johannesburg 2196,
South Africa
Penguin Books Ltd., Registered Offices: 80 Strand, London WC2R 0RL, England

While the author has made every effort to provide accurate telephone numbers and Internet addresses at the time of publication, neither the publisher nor the author assumes any responsibility for errors or for changes that occur after publication. Further, the publisher does not have any control over and does not assume any responsibility for author or third-party websites or their content.

Copyright © 2011 by Eva Christina
Text design by Tiffany Estreicher
Illustrations by Michael Lotenero

First edition: October 2011

Library of Congress Cataloging-in-Publication Data

Christina, Eva.
    The book of kink : sex beyond the missionary / Eva Christina.— 1st ed.
       p.   cm.
    ISBN 978-0-399-53694-6
    1. Sex—History—21st century.   2. Sex customs—History—21st century.   I. Title.
    HQ21.C527   2011
    306.77—dc23   2011018724

PRINTED IN THE UNITED STATES OF AMERICA

10 9 8 7 6 5 4 3 2

Most Perigee books are available at special quantity discounts for bulk purchases for sales promotions, premiums, fund-raising, or educational use. Special books, or book excerpts, can also be created to fit specific needs. For details, write: Special Markets, Penguin Group (USA) Inc., 375 Hudson Street, New York, New York 10014.

To K&A,
for giving me all my body parts

ACKNOWLEDGMENTS

Huge thanks to my agent, Andrea Somberg—there's no other way to say it: I couldn't be in better hands. I'm also extremely thankful to Maria Gagliano, my superb editor who offered such expert advice every step of the way, and to everyone else at Penguin for their support.

So many others to thank . . . Carly for her wealth of information and contacts; Lexa for all her research; to those who gave me their time to interview them: Kevin Blatt, Dr. Ava Cadell, Christy Canyon, Master Feenix, Adam Grayson, Farrell Hirsch, Nikki Hunter, Larry Flynt, Theresa Flynt, Matt McMullen, Christian Mann, Dana B. Myers, Miss Nikki Nefarious, Goddess Soma, Ariel Joseph Towne, and the friends, family and contacts who all helped in one way or another, either in support and/or to make sure I got the kinkiest of material: Brian Gross, Amanda Thompson, Erin Palmquist, the Kinsey Institute, the S-Factor, Sara, Patty, Jess and JP, Alexa and Pancho, Tina, Joyce, Erin and Randy, Agnieszka, Cybele, Robynn, Clara, Charles, Tom and John, Carla, Shola, Diane, Charles, Tanya, Davide, Violetta, Tomasz, Lowry,

Logan, Adam, Eline and Scott, Dyanne and Matt, Agatha, Sonia, Adam and Sara, and Alex.

No book about kinky sex could have a better muse than the daily reflections from the *Howard Stern Show*. I want to thank Stern for his wild and incisive shows, providing me with great leads on sexy and kinky ideas. More media thanks to Gawker, the *Daily Beast* and the *Huffington Post*—somehow, these sites seemed to have something relevant to my book almost every day.

Lastly, I could not be more grateful to my parents for being so much a part of my life every single day and for all that they do, have done and continue to do; my gorgeous daughters, who take my breath away—but won't be allowed to read this book for a very long time; and my husband, who with all his sexiness, smartness and hilarity, is even hotter in his endless support, and as my own collaborator, confidant and comfort.

CONTENTS

INTRODUCTION

What do Marv Albert, Paris Hilton and Adolf Hitler have in common? I'll give you a hint: it has nothing to do with basketball, bad singing or brownshirts. These three famous yet completely dissimilar people have been into wild, crazy, uninhibited and kinky sex. In the public eye, they are known as a classy sports announcer, a spoiled heiress and a murderous dictator. But once you get them behind closed doors, these three—and millions of others—make doggy-style look like Disneyland. Whether you're gnawing on a woman's back like a botfly, making a homemade tape while giving fellatio with a night-vision camera or lying between an upright woman's legs while you paint her vagina, people everywhere are into kinky sex. For some, it's a way to spice up a withered sex life; for others, it's a lifestyle. No matter how or why you engage in kinky sex, let it be known that it is as old as Adam and Eve and as commonplace as your next-door neighbor.

Why do people engage in such erotic, titillating and naughty behavior? What is it about kinkiness that makes a person risk their career and family to self-indulge for just a few hours? Why would a store clerk risk sex with a mannequin in public? Why does the timid payroll manager at your office rush home on Thursdays because she's hosting "brothel night"? Why does a hedge fund CEO want to be flogged? Why does a conservative housewife want her hair pulled? Is it in our blood? Our genes? Are our lives that boring that we have to supplement the private moments with behavior that is often uncharacteristic of who we portray ourselves to be in public? Can we control the urge? Do we need to? We seem to have kinkiness everywhere, and what's kinky to one person is completely different from what's kinky to another.

But if it's really everywhere, why is kinky sex still so taboo?

Just like our infatuation with celebrities, kinky sex is something we all wish for but never think is within reach. And it's forever intriguing. Even the word "kinky" sounds kinky. It's a word that evokes a secretive, sexy and sultry curiosity. We'll never stop being curious. It's part of our nature. Many of us are already extremely curious about other people's sex lives. Without other people's sex lives, well, what the hell would we all talk about? How would tabloids stay afloat? Why would we care about "Brangelina"? If sex is part of our national fabric, kinky is the stain on that proverbial textile that no one wants to talk about but is impossible to "cleanse."

The word "kinky" is used to define an act or object that is grossly racy or raunchy, gratuitously taboo or titillating, secretly lewd or obscene. In 1992, the Diagnostic and Statistical Manual of Mental Disorders, a manual that's published by the American Psychiatric Association on mental disorders and how to refer to them, defined "kinky behavior" as "paraphilia"—whatever act or idea is abnormally used to get someone aroused. The same manual classified homosexuality as a mental health issue until 1974.

Today, kinky sex has turned in a more positive direction. Have our standards fallen? Have we moved the goalposts for what is deemed coarse or crude or too sexy? We live in a world where a movie showing someone masturbating into an apple pie becomes a box-office smash. When Madonna grabs her crotch onstage, she has countless teenybopper girls emulating her every move. Bruce Willis can prove his love for his new wife by being photographed in *W* magazine donning S&M attire. Geriatric sex guru Dr. Ruth Westheimer spewed out the most shocking—yet informative—sex advice. People pay to see Britney Spears dress as a dominatrix in one of her concerts. Books about having a year without sex or a woman's quest to have an orgasm are top sellers. And Chris Rock makes the "art" of tossing salad funny.

The Book of Kink will take bedroom doors off of their hinges, not peeking into the world of kinkiness but exposing it. If you've never heard the terms or engaged in the practice of strap-ons, flagellation, sword fighting, rough-putting or the Sybian, this book is about to take your innocence and pop its cherry.

The book will be like a multi-camera porn shoot. We'll look at every possible angle, from the history, how-tos and hilarity of kinkiness—and yet it will only really scratch the surface on a subject that is enormously vast, dense and populated. Some close-up framing might cause a bit of discomfort, but most of these looks will be money shots, eye-opening focal points on the details of kinky behavior. It will discuss equipment, classes, parties and porn. It will delve into fetishes, turn-ons, role-playing and how the Internet has reinvented how kinky people find one another. It will look at why we are kinky, whether we humans were always kinky, and what it means to be kinky. It'll look back at historical personas and cultures who were kinky (Did Attila the Hun's seventh wife kill him with rough and rugged sex? Did you know the ancient Egyptians masturbated in groups in order to make sure their fields were fertile?). The book will peep into the world of celebrity and political scandals, like ex–New York governor Eliot Spitzer's desire to have sex with high-priced hookers. It will discuss laws and scrutinize what happens when this kind of activity goes wrong.

Studies on kinky practices today are harder than ever to find because not only is it difficult to raise money for that kind of research, but it's even harder to get people to be honest. Statistics vary wildly on what percentage of the population indulges in kinky sex, with 5 to 50 percent saying they're kinky, which means there's a huge margin of error. On top of that, people's various definitions of kinkiness factor into the equation and can throw the entire survey out the window.

Whether it's to find your own definition of kink, to spice up your relationship or just to let curiosity take over, let's shake things up and investigate what's *beyond* the missionary.

THE BOOK OF
Kink

One

KINK GONE MAINSTREAM

The only unnatural sexual act is that which you cannot perform.   —ALFRED KINSEY

You're skimming the news and are totally engrossed in an article about a conservative preacher who has always championed traditional marriage. Now he's been found with two men who were ramming him with a rolling pin, and let's just say it was consensual. You don't know what fascinates you more: that all this time the hypocrite has been secretly gay or that, *Wow!* he's into some kinky play.

Maybe you've been dating this woman and you're thinking: *I've been a gentleman long enough. Tonight in bed, I'm going to stick my thumb in her tush.* The time is right. The lights are low and the music is romantic. You're in a sensual embrace and you're about to do something with your thumb that you would never tell you grandmother about. You take a deep breath before going in. Then, suddenly, you feel your anal sphincter flinch. She's putting her thumb in your tush! Kinky!

You're hanging with your lover one night, flipping through the TV channels. He stops on porn, which you never watch. He does jumping jacks with his eyebrows, hoping to spark interest. You decide to actually take a look. You've always viewed pornography as sick, twisted, gross, degrading, raunchy, horny, sexy, wet, hot . . . Holy crap, you're getting turned on. He raises the remote and feigns changing the channel, hoping you'll tell him to wait. You tell him to leave it for a second.

Does this mean you're kinky?

Some say kinky is only kinky when you're engaging in sexual behavior outside of your comfort zone for the first time. After that, it may *become* the norm. It's just another facet of your sex life. So is kinky all whips and chains, handcuffs, hot wax, latex, bondage and stilettos? Sure, but only to a degree. There's a lot of creativity that goes into kinky.

What many people consider to be kinky today is simply sexual activity that's been around since the dawn of man. The ebb and flow of what's considered appropriate sex versus kinky sex has always gone through phases. But it appears as though more and more once-deemed-kinky activities are being viewed as sexually or socially acceptable. The mainstreaming of kinky sex has been evolving and will continue to progress, pushing some people's moral compasses in a new direction while others find themselves thriving in this new openness. Dr. Ava Cadell, founder and president of Loveology University, puts it like this: "If love makes the world go round, sex is what keeps it on course." I suppose kinky sex is what steers it into new directions.

What Is the Missionary Position?

The missionary is one of the most familiar sexual positions in today's world. The man is on top, penetrating the woman who is lying beneath him, legs spread. The man does most of the work, with the woman not really even needing to participate except for making sure her legs are spread wide enough to allow for ease of entry. In some cultures and religions, such as the Islamic world, this is the only position that is acceptable for a woman to engage in. It is also the only "acceptable" position in Washington, DC, where any other position is considered illegal. Most people consider the missionary to be vanilla sex, with no wild side at all. It's just plain and bland like yogurt. It might be enough for many sexually active people, but when others try new positions, games and fun, it leaves them only wanting more. Sort of like adding granola to that yogurt.

The Mainstreaming of Kink

The line of what's kinky is very gray these days. Not too long ago, lingerie was considered a fetish and taboo. Sexy exposure like a bare ankle was once a big turn-on. Today, it's no big deal to see a model on a poster spanning New York City's Times Square in nothing but a tiny G-string. As Farrell Hirsch, head of Playboy Radio, bluntly explains, "When I was twelve, no one said 'fuck' on TV. Now, people fuck on TV."

Pornography has helped make kinky sex mainstream. *Taboo* magazine's Ernest Greene (and husband to porn legend, sex educator and author Nina Hartley) drove the point home in a 2010 AlterNet.org article called "Kinky Sex: When Did BDSM Become So Wildly Popular?" "Eventually," says Greene, "we'll reach a point where bondage in a porn movie is no more controversial than a blow job." Christian Mann, general manager of the porn production and distribution company Evil Angel, adds to that in an interview: "It's interesting to me that people on the outer edges of the sexual frontiers, given enough time, always wind up influencing the mainstream. With the mainstream, it's become very vanilla. Soccer moms are all getting their tramp stamps (a lower back tattoo)."

The numbers of those actually into kinky sex are only rising, and that's largely thanks to the Internet, which has changed the name of the kinky game entirely. Looking for a chat room dedicated to women who are addicted to the "rabbit"? Go here. Need a website that sells nurses' uniforms? Click on this link. The World Wide Web makes kinky a cinch. Whether you're into the leather world, Latino swingers or paddle nightclubs, you can find it all. You just have to find the proverbial reproductive organs to take the leap. Books on BDSM (bondage and discipline, dominance and submission, sadism and masochism) are now coming out, such as

Whip Smart by Melissa Febos, who describes her life as a New York City dominatrix. Online communities are flourishing as more people decide to log in and meet like-minded people. Just check out Fetlife.com, the largest social network for people into kink, fetishes and BDSM. Most people find the anonymous factor on the Internet to be a huge turn-on, but there are also countless events and parties you can attend (and find out about online), such as the Deaf Leather contest, the Black Rose convention (Washington, DC) and Beat Me in St. Louis.

What's in Pop?

Pop culture has also had a huge influence on the "outing" of sex beyond the missionary and pushing the balance of what's "acceptable" sexually and what's not. And my, how times have changed. In 1947, Mary Kay and Johnny (in the TV show by the same name) were supposed to be in bed together—we just never saw them. It wasn't until 1960 when Fred and Wilma Flintstone became the first TV couple to be shown in bed together. Today, we have a dominatrix cracking pistachios in TV commercials for a campaign called "Get Crackin'." Paris Hilton is on all fours in a dental floss swimsuit eating a huge cheeseburger. Singer Rihanna put out an S&M music video as a means to make fun of the mass media. The music video featured "reporters" wearing ball gags and getting whipped, while she sang all geared up in latex. And although banned, Eva Mendes came close to writhing around on a bed naked and briefly exposing a nipple for Calvin Klein. Needless to say, this ain't your grandmother's marketing strategy.

Pop has taken kinkiness to a new level, making it "cool" and even profitable. When Diana Rigg pulled on that tight black leather catsuit in the *Avengers* TV show, the attire instantly became a fashion fetish. When Sharon Stone used those silk scarves to tie up her lovers in the thriller *Basic Instinct*, $195 white silk Hermès scarves jumped in sales.

But what many people appreciate is that with the Internet, television and film bringing sex to the foreground, people are realizing they're not alone with their desires. Not only are we finding connections to others online, but even the most popular figures in sports, politics and entertainment are getting "caught" in kinky acts.

It's rumored singer John Mayer is the kinky type and is constantly needing to sharpen the blade that makes the notches in his bedpost because his lovers fall hard for his bedroom antics. Sting was said to talk up Tantric sex (the yoga that originated in India, where sex brings a person closer to enlightenment), giving the

Kidman's Kinkiness

Actress Nicole Kidman shocked the world when she said this in a 2009 *GQ* magazine interview: "I've explored obsession . . . I've explored strange sexual fetish stuff, I've explored the mundane aspect of marriage, and monogamy."

activity a seal of approval—but then acknowledged it was a joke. And there are TV shows exploring sex like TLC's *Strange Sex*, HBO's *Real Sex* and the History Channel's *History of Sex*.

KINKINESS AND THE CITY

HBO's *Sex and the City* figured out what women want on the TV screen, especially in bedroom scenes. The plotlines included countless fetishes, positions and sexual freedoms. Women all over the world converged on Sunday nights to watch and live vicariously through Carrie, Samantha, Charlotte and Miranda. The show became so popular, a British woman named Christina Saunders decided she wanted to emulate the character of Samantha and made it a personal quest to sleep with 1,000 guys; that's exactly what she did during the next ten years, trying to bed at least one guy a week. According to *News of the World*, she told them in 2010 that "I wanted to be confident like [Samantha]. I got hooked on the buzz of one-night stands." After she succeeded, she thinks she may have gone "too far. Now all I want to do is settle down."

THE PRINTED KINK

The print world is part of this kinky media storm. Of course, magazines like *Playboy*, *Penthouse* and *Hustler* have created movements that have attracted a loyal army of readers. And then there are those magazines that are considered "PG" and just dishing out "acceptable" (as in, nothing too risqué) sex advice, such as encouraging "outercourse" (nonpenetrative sex that involves anything

Spying Kink

Anna Chapman, a famous Russian spy who was caught in 2010, became all the rage not only because of her sexy looks, but because of exes coming out and detailing her sexual escapades. There were stories in the media filled with naked photographs, mile-high sex, sex marathons and her penchant for sex toys, making James Bonds's vixens look sheepish.

However, Chapman still pales in comparison to Hana Koecher, who worked in the United States for the communist Czechoslovakia's intelligence service (under KGB supervision) in the 1980s. In her later years, after she was one of the spies swapped for Natan Sharansky (a prominent Soviet dissident who was accused of spying for the United States and sentenced for more than a decade to a Siberian labor camp), she bragged about bedding countless CIA and Pentagon employees, plus journalists and even a senator. She and her husband, Karl, also met for group sex once a week at a swingers club called Capitol Couples. When the sex party organizer was asked about them later, he was quoted in Ronald Kessler's book *Spy vs. Spy* as saying, "I found them an interesting couple. He was a professor. She was a diamond merchant . . . Incredibly orgasmic. I went to bed with her several times. But I thought Karl was a bit strange . . . He was always naked at the parties. Usually people keep their clothes on at least some of the time, but he was always walking around naked. And he always had an erection."

Spies of course do need to investigate every possible situation that could have secrets, as unlikely as it may seem.

from erotic talk to frottage to mutual masturbation as a way of curbing STDs and pregnancy), or *Self* magazine, which explains "sex pyramids" (like "food pyramids," these pyramids explain the importance of changing your diet of sex, from going solo to introducing electricity to make-up sex). But these mainstream magazines are also turning up the heat. *Interview* magazine put actress Blake Lively on the cover in handcuffs. You have the threesome of actors from the HBO series *True Blood* naked and smeared with blood on the cover of *Rolling Stone* magazine. Khloe Kardashian showed up on the cover of *YRB* magazine in an S&M mask. And Scarlett Johansson posed with burlesque dancer Dita von Teese in S&M bondage scenes for *Flaunt* magazine.

Sex Ed

Male strippers used to be the norm at bachelorette parties. While they still come in handy, nowadays a bachelorette party isn't exciting or unique if it doesn't have a "blow job" specialist giving lessons on a zucchini or a banana. Today's bachelorette parties also entertain with a classically trained dancer who will teach the attendees how to strip for their lovers. Just doing a round of "pin the penis on the groom" doesn't cut it anymore.

Sexual education classes are catering to packed audiences everywhere. Topics range from "incorporating uniforms" to "fisting for fun" to "introducing the Cleveland Steamer." Famous sexperts give lectures titled, for example, "Rope Bondage Dojo," by Midori, at places like the nationwide sex-toy store the Pleasure Chest (which, according to its website, helped "launch the original sex toy boutique"); "Making Spaces for Sex: From Rituals to Parties to Playa" by Carol Queen at the 2010 Arse Elektronika in San Francisco; and in Annie Sprinkle's case, a screening of "Annie Sprinkle's Amazing World of Orgasm" at places like Ohio University or the countless other colleges where she has had lectures and screenings.

LOVEOLOGY

Dr. Ava Cadell has taken sex education classes to a whole new level. She is the founder of Loveology University, a university entirely dedicated to love and sex. The online higher education center has an array of classes, with course stages that range from levels one to four. Why she felt it was important to start a "loveology" university is probably best answered by her: "Sex is the most important subject for everybody to learn . . . I think that the meaning of life is learning how to give and receive love. In the end, nothing is going to matter as much as the loving memories that you have. You're not going to focus on the amount of money you made or the job you had, it's going to be about love, it's going to be about intimacy. I just think that it's powerful energy. There's nothing that makes us happier or sadder than love." Dr. Cadell adds to her comments in an interview, "I think sex is one of the most beautiful gifts you can give to somebody who's worthy of it."

Studying has never been this fun or this hot. Level one courses include Masturbation, Guides to Flirting and Dating, and 12 Steps to Everlasting Love. Level two classes focus on passion and intimacy: Guides to What Men/Women Want in Bed, Passion Power for Couples, and Oral Sex. Stepping up to level three, students will find courses on Aphrodisiacs and Sensual Massage as well as the G-Spot Tutorial and Venus Butterfly. The fourth and final level takes a closer look at subjects ranging from the Tantric Workbook to Parental Concerns. When asked whom the university is geared toward, Cadell says, "I want people from all walks of life, genders and cultures to be able to learn and yet I want it to be on a level that whether you're a beginner or advanced, you get something out of it. I love to help empower people to have the best sex of their lives. And that includes kinky sex."

Students can graduate as Romantics, Master Sexperts and certified Loveologist Love Coaches through the university. A Romantic is one who knows dating, flirting, foreplay and massage. A Master Sexpert is what it sounds like: a graduate who knows everything about sex. And the Love Coach is "the evolution of a life coach," claims Dr. Cadell. "It's someone who coaches you about your love life. So they can help you with your dating issues, with your breakup issues. They're not therapists but they can certainly help you find love or help you become more sexually confident between the sheets and introduce you to new, fun love lessons."

THE LIFE OF A PORN STAR . . . CAN BE YOURS

"Porn Star Sex Life" was a tutorial offered in person in New York City in both 2009 and 2010 by Penthouse Pet Ryan Keely. The mission of the all-day seminar was to help people find their inner porn star, which of course will result in better sex. And there are plenty of other workshops by different sex educators that teach you porn, BDSM and other activities, such as Tantric sex weekends; the Training of O (where women take a four-day slave-training course); Rough and Tumble: An Evening for Rough and Sexy Take-down Play (at the Center for Sex Positive Culture); and Sex Bondage Safety. Not your average study session but something you'll no doubt remember well.

BOOTY PARLOR

For many people, visiting sex stores can feel like walking into the opposite sex's public bathroom: You feel out of place and there's potential to see private parts. It feels dirty and risky, and a lot of products look scary. Enter Booty Parlor. Launched in 2005, they've got sex products at the Wynn Las Vegas, VictoriasSecret.com and various other places. Their products are not only inviting; they're enticing. Dana B. Myers, who co-owns Booty Parlor with her husband, Charlie, says her goal was to create a sensual beauty line: "Booty Parlor's philosophy is to create products that boost a woman's sexy self-confidence and inspire her to create sexier experiences both in and out of the bedroom." Now shopping for clothes, makeup and sex accessories can blend easily together, making the experience fun and exciting—not awkward and scary.

Booty Parlor has six distinct categories of products: seductive beauty, romantic treats, bedroom accessories, love kits, sexy lingerie and sex toys. Eye-catchers include Good Girl/Bad Girl Wrist

Cuffs (soft leather cuffs with ruffles that are sensuous and daring at the same time) and Turn Me On Vibrating Panties (remote-controlled so he can turn you on while you mingle separately at a party).

A growing part of their business is their Booty Parlor Sexy Shopping Parties (think Tupperware parties with an NC-17 twist). They have around 700 sexy lifestyle advisors nationwide conducting these parties. "Women come to us," Myers explains. "They buy a business kit, they become a sexy lifestyle advisor, they get their own personal website to run their business, they have access training, events, and the like, and then they go out in their communities and it's word of mouth." The lifestyle advisors come to your home and show off the line—and educate you at the same time. Celebs like Jennifer Love Hewitt and Tori Spelling have indulged.

BABELAND

Babeland has a chain of sex-toy stores nationwide. Not only do they sell all types of sex gadgets, but they also offer classes. In one class, students were taught how to recycle old bicycle tires and turn them into their own flogs. They even demonstrate at the end of class to make sure the transformed flogging instruments are working right. Other classes available include Erotic Bondage, Dominatrix Worship, the Art of the Blow Job and Dirty Talk. And at some stores, there's a free Sunday brunch and Cheap Date Nights to encourage more couples to come together.

HIGH-END SEX

Coco de Mer is known for its high-class toys and clientele, with locations in New York, Los Angeles and London. They offer salons—carried over from eighteenth-century rituals—that gather for "Hands on Rope Bondage" by renowned sexpert Midori.

Kink 101 is a class at Coco de Mer but sponsored by Domi Dollz, an organization founded by Kimi Inch with the goal that it "revamps and elevates the Kinky Scene, bringing it to the mainstream in a daring and fun manner," according to its website. Kink 101 has a leather-clad teacher instruct on the basics of life as a dominatrix, and how to spice up the bedroom with tricks. And it's just one of the various classes and workshops Domi Dollz puts on, with others—such as dominatrix Domina K's Art of Partner Play—being offered in venues such as the upscale and luxurious Kiki de Monteparnasse sex store. Inch and her fellow Domi Dollz tour the world and offer their expertise, talents and seduction to thousands. Their T-shirts with two simple words on them— "Yes, Mistress"—are quite popular.

HUSTLIN' *HUSTLER*

The Hustler sex stores were birthed with Larry Flynt's vision of "creating a store that even a schoolteacher would feel comfortable coming into." Some of their bestselling items are vibrating cock rings from Screaming O (they're inexpensive and disposable) and high-end products including Liberator pillows (a pillow made specifically for sex positions). They have occasional workshops where a person can learn anything from pole dancing to strip tease. And the Sunset Boulevard store in Los Angeles has an enticing, sexy café. When speaking of how kinkiness is becoming more mainstream, Theresa Flynt, Larry Flynt's daughter and executive vice president of Flynt Media Corporation, pointed out the increase in fetish products available at the company's iconic Hustler Hollywood retail stores. "The fetish section has grown significantly from year to year. Fetish is a niche market. So at Hustler Hollywood, we mainly sell to those who are beginners in Fetish . . . the furry handcuffs, a simple blindfold, feather ticklers, that sort of thing."

PINUPS

Pinup girls were all the rage in the early 1900s, with models and actresses being photographed in tempting attire, an overabundance of makeup and suggestive poses revealing a sliver of skin (also known as "cheesecake" photography). Pinup queen and legendary cult figure Bettie Page was the quintessential pinup, gracing *Playboy* as Miss January 1955, and doing things like putting a kinky, S&M twist on many of her photos.

Today, women are sexifying themselves by emulating pinup greats such as Page, Betty Grable, Veronica Lake and Marilyn Monroe. Programs like the Pin Up Finishing School in New York City are soaring in popularity. Here, women of all shapes, sizes, colors and ages can learn how to be a pinup girl or just look like one. They take classes on how to always be glamorous and, according to the website, to be that "confident, sassy, sexy gal with the twinkle in her eye."

SHAGGING IN SHAG

Shag in Brooklyn, New York, is an erotic boutique, studio and gallery, with everything from performances to exhibits to classes. The Shaggin' Mama Moves workshop focuses on getting new mothers back in the groove by doing things like pelvic exercises, and the Instructional Body Painting workshop gives women and men a whole new canvas to work with.

FINDING YOUR SEXY SPIRIT

Richard Anton Diaz is founder of Sexy Spirits, a New York institution that, according to its website, is "dedicated to the education and cultivation of sexual energy." Students are taught how to have longer-lasting orgasms, prevent premature ejaculation and engage in unique sex practices. Diaz, a former dancer, also teaches Tantra Tango, where students learn sensuality with their dance partners. Seminars with live demonstrations on orgasms are also available.

GOING FOR THAT ONE TASTE

OneTaste Urban Retreat Center, located in both San Francisco and New York, is a community of people who live and breathe orgasms—in particular, female orgasms. They live in a commune where they practice yoga and meditation, and lead sexuality workshops. Every morning, they wake to focus on orgasmic mediation, where the women lie half-naked and the men put their skills to the test to make them come.

Coaching sessions from Slow Sex Meetup to the Art of Orgasmic Meditation are some of what's available. The founder, Nicole Daedone, explained in a 2009 *New York Times* article called "The Pleasure Principle" that women can truly find freedom when "they own their sexuality," and her goal was to put together a sexual "mindfulness" center—with the added bonus of long orgasms. Although some people think of OneTaste as more of a cult, not many can argue that participants are truly getting off on it.

Ms. Daedone's mentor is Ray Vetterlein, the hero of the extended female orgasm. He's the legendary man who figured out a way to make a woman's orgasm last a good twenty minutes!

DIPLOMAS IN SEXUALITY

College years are often a time of serious self-exploration. But to some, it's sex-ploration. Since 2005, Yale University has been holding an annual sex week, where students are given an education of a different sort. From sex-toy raffles and speed dating to speaking with porn stars and taking BDSM 101, this student-run awareness week has been successful and controversial while promoting safe sexuality and healthy sex awareness. (Yale's prank group called the Pundit held its annual naked party in early 2011. But several students ended up in the hospital, and there was even an allegation that a sexual assault had occurred.)

Yale isn't the only higher education institution hopping in the proverbial sack with sex awareness. Northwestern University, the University of Kentucky and Brown University have their own sex weeks. Brown University's sex week kicks off with a documentary called *Kink*.

And at Skidmore College, a how-to masturbation guide was posted in campus restrooms for all students to read. Published by the college's Center for Sex and Gender Relations, the guide was called the "Your-Body-Is-a-Wonderland Edition," and suggests getting off on your own will help you deal with exam stress.

But sometimes, educational sex exhibitions don't go exactly as planned. At Northwestern University, psychology professor J. Michael Bailey had to apologize after showing a live sex demonstration in his human sexuality class. A woman allowed her boyfriend to insert a "fucksaw," or a sawlike device with a phallic top (in-

Transcendent Sex

There are those who believe in transcendent sex, which essentially means they are having mystical, out-of-body experiences, time travel, past lives and other mind-blowing reactions during a hop in the sack. This oftentimes comes spontaneously out of nowhere. Dr. Jenny Wade even wrote the book *Transcendent Sex: When Lovemaking Opens the Veil*, about these spiritual and altered states of consciousness during sex, which Wade calls "one of the best-kept secrets in human history."

stead of a blade), inside of her. According to one student, she grabbed the mic to explain how she got turned on by having crowds watch her. The rest of the class discussion focused on kinky sex and the female orgasm. Interactive studying at its best.

Thinking Off

I can actually mentally give myself an orgasm. You know, sense memory is quite powerful. —LADY GAGA IN *NEW YORK* MAGAZINE

When they say sex is all about the mind, a "thinking off" orgasm truly embodies the notion. There are people who believe—and teach—that one can have an orgasm without being touched. And people such as New York–based sex educator Barbara Carrellas have proven to scientists that the same brain activity that happens during an orgasm happens with "thinking off" (or "energy orgasm" as it's sometimes called). Carrellas, who finessed this talent

Hormones

A study at the University of Pisa, Italy, revealed that people's attraction to one another lasted only the first two years of a relationship. After that, a different hormone takes over—oxytocin, which is the "cuddling hormone." So maybe a bit of kink can help pick things back up.

in the eighties as a response to the AIDS epidemic, even teaches classes on how to master this technique. People lie around in a circle on the floor, close their eyes and, with no genital touching, get into it as Carrellas "walks" them through the process by talking to them. Sometimes it takes fantasizing; sometimes it takes concentrating on one's breathing and energy. Whichever way it happens, Carrellas claims the release can come.

Sexercise

Exercise can come in all different shapes and forms: tae bo, yoga, Pilates. Now people have figured out that the one of the best forms of exercise can be a combination of both—sex and calisthenics.

THE POLE

Pole-dancing classes have become very popular. This arousing, erotic dance not only gets you feeling, acting and moving sexy, it gets you in shape. Sheila Kelley's S Factor is just one nationwide chain that keeps expanding and responding to the growing demand for classes. The chain was created to empower women, and those who enroll find the classes to be tough, sexy and fun. As Sheila Kelley says on her website, "S Factor was born when I discovered my sensual power and the best body of my life while preparing for my role as an exotic dancer. My life changed so profoundly just from moving in this organically feminine way that I've dedicated myself to sharing this extraordinary journey with other women."

These dancing classes have spread far and wide, with various companies opening their own versions. Celebrities have fallen in love with the pole so much that they've even set them up in their own homes. Jennifer Love Hewitt has admitted to having one in her house and being part of her workout routine in a 2010 conference call with the *Huffington Post*. Martha Stewart took a spin on a pole on national TV. And many actresses have mastered the pole for film roles: Lindsay Lohan, Heather Graham, Demi Moore, Marisa Tomei, Natalie Portman and Salma Hayek. Oprah has featured the exercise on her show. Turns out, sometimes the simple things are all it takes—and a simple metal rod can create a whole lotta sexy.

There's even a magazine devoted to pole dancing called *Pole Spin*. And there are also plenty of stripping classes available as well, which don't include a pole. They teach you similar sensual movements—and, of course, how to take off your clothes in a way no lover will forget.

BELLY DANCING

Despite its name, this seductive Middle Eastern dance is all about the hips. It's an art form that's been around for thousands of years. Belly dancing began as a way to celebrate fertility or a young woman's entrance into marriage, and it was a dance done mostly in front of other women, not men. It didn't take long for men to discover these sexy movements, and soon enough they demanded to be entertained by belly dancers as well.

Belly dancing came to the United States by way of the Chicago World's Fair in 1893, when a dancer known as Little Egypt shook up audiences with her pelvic thrusts, rhythmic music and sexuality. Today, belly-dancing classes, workshops and festivals are commonplace, and studies even reveal that associated pelvic movements help blood stimulation into the region, which can turn up a woman's libido, balance hormones and help with things like PMS.

BURLESQUE

Burlesque dancing is a sensual, sexual dance that usually ends with a striptease. Classes are wildly popular, as are burlesque shows around the world. As Augusta Avallone, founder of a burlesque school called the Striptease Symposium, says in a 2010 *Los Angeles Times* article, "Most women wouldn't go to a strip club, but burlesque is more accessible because of the glamour, fashion and playfulness." The 2010 movie *Burlesque* with Cher and Christina Aguilera is testament to its continuing popularity.

One of the first things that usually comes to mind about burlesque are the costumes—as it should. The attire is key, a mishmash of Victorian undergarment attire with bad-girl elements. This was a huge contrast to Victorian-era England, which was a time when women were forced to hide every part of their body. But the performance group the British Blondes, headed by Lydia

Thompson, who slid into some scandalous tights and performed onstage burlesque dance for the first time in the United States in 1868, daringly took off some layers, exposing much more than was socially acceptable. They were a huge hit, especially after critics openly condemned this form of dance as indecent. What's that they say about bad publicity? The dance really became hot in the late 1800s, especially in how it made fun of the opera, theater and ballet for working class audiences, and Mabel Saintley became America's first homegrown burlesque dancer. Burlesque producers the Minsky brothers got Gypsy Rose Lee onstage on Broadway and she too was a huge hit. But because stripping started to become popular and devalued burlesque's initial intent, the last burlesque house closed in New York in 1937. That didn't mean it was forgotten. Some of the biggest women in burlesque were Lili St. Cyr and Millie DeLeon, and today, Dita von Teese is the most famous classical burlesque dancer. Burlesque dancers attempted to break the record of the largest burlesque dance in London's Trafalgar Square in early 2011, giving tourists some more spectacular views of the city.

CIRCUS TRICKS

The circus is a popular form of entertainment. These days, performers seem to be adding more spice to their routines with nudity, fetishes and sex. La Clique (called La Soirée as of 2010) made a name for itself at the Edinburgh Fringe Festival in 2004, and has plenty of fantasy and fetish going on in its sexy cabaret/

variety show combination. New Zealand's Heavenly Burlesque has strippers join the circus performers to give a mix of safe and provocative entertainment. In Cirque du Soleil's 2003 Las Vegas show *Zumanity*, incredibly talented dancers are put to the test of stripping down and moving their bodies in extreme ways, all with obvious erotic overtones (its final number is a massive orgy). And at a nightclub like La Fee Verte (the Green Fairy) in Miami, Florida, not only can you catch a burlesque show; you can also see circus aerial performances, which are steamy-hot and death-defying.

Even celebrities are catching on. Carmen Electra claimed in 2006 on NBC's *Tonight Show* that she was going to install an aerial circus hoop in her house so that she could do X-rated circus tricks for an audience of one: her husband.

Jazzle Up Your Snazzle

There are countless things you can do to spice up your body. To-day's hottest trends in body beautification include surgical gloves and operating rooms (designer vaginas or vaginoplasty), machines (penis lengthening), coloring (the pink wink—code for "anal bleaching") and sometimes, just a little bit of glue, glitter and creativity.

VAJAZZLE

The term "vajazzle" officially entered the English lexicon when actress Jennifer Love Hewitt admitted to having what looked like a "disco ball" between her legs while on the *Lopez Tonight* show on TBS in 2010. It looks like it sounds. Imagine taking some gems and affixing them to your vagina . . . that's pretty much vajazzling, except there are no clamps or brass hooks. After a wax, the interested party can stick Swarovski crystals onto their private area into a decorative formation, such as a flower, arrow or word. Painless, the gems will usually stick around for five days. The New York City spa Completely Bare was one of the first places to start the practice and has been busy creating these sparkling designs on women ever since. Not visiting NYC anytime soon? Completely Bare offers a do-it-yourself package, with an online tutorial and shipment of the gems.

TATS

Before vajazzling, another way to decorate a woman's privates was to get a tattoo. Twattoo or Va-ttoo is permanent or temporary ink designed in a certain formation above, next to or around the genitals. Using her pubic hair, one lady designed a bearded man around her woman area.

SPA-GINA

Thinking of sprucing up your private parts? Koreans have been known for their tradition of offering vagina day spas, where a lady can get a different type of "facial" (called *chai-yok*). Using a combination of mugwort tea, wormwood and other herbs in a boiling pot of hot water, women sit naked above these concoctions, which are thought to help regulate menstrual periods, clear infections and hemorrhoids, and reduce stress. And Americans are taking notice. For example, Tikkun Holistic Spa in Santa Monica, California, has now opened its own vag-spas, offering a similar steam cleaning.

MEN'S PLAY

Men have also been known to jazz up their penises with tattoos, piercings and other creative ornaments. But an even more fun—or at least tasty—project is the "Clone-a-Willy" kit. Men can make a mold of their member in chocolate, candy or lollipop form. But ladies, don't worry; there's also a "Clone-a-Pussy" kit. Get a replica of your privates and turn it into edible fun.

Age Kink

Age has always stirred curiosity, especially in our youth-obsessed society. Whether it's "cougars," "MILFs" ("Mother I'd Like to Fuck") or "jailbait," age has always been a pivotal attribute of kinky.

Men have always wanted younger women; in all societies, they are equated with fertility. But now more women are making it socially acceptable to date younger men. Studies such as a 2010 one by University of Texas at Austin professor of psychology David Buss have revealed that women between the ages of twenty-seven and forty-five are the horniest they'll ever be, due to their bodies realizing that they've got to step up their libido if they want to make a baby at a later stage. On the contrary, a man's sexual high point is in his teens. So it makes sense that older women want younger men. A 2003 AARP study showed that 30 percent of American women over forty were dating younger men. However, British psychologists conducted a 2010 study in which they found that most women still do want to find someone their own age or older, and not prey on younger men as the media likes to claim.

Studies also reveal that men have more sex than women later in life, with men still getting it on in their seventies, while women are usually much less interested in sex after menopause. Women, don't lose all hope, though. A report from the website the Sex eZine states that 30 percent of women over eighty still know their way around under the sheets.

With celebrity couples like Demi Moore and Ashton Kutcher— with a fifteen-year difference in their ages—"cougars" have become as fashionable as sex tapes. So fashionable, in fact, that Courteney Cox took a stab at a TV show called *Cougar Town*, where she plays a divorcée who gets back in the dating world, dating guys who sometimes might be closer to her teenage son's age, who happens to still be living at home with her. In real life, she was married to David Arquette, who was seven years her junior. Madonna,

Cher, Susan Sarandon and Linda Hogan are just a few others who have also scored big in the cougar category. But, of course, the original cougar is the character of Mrs. Robinson (played by Anne Bancroft), in the movie *The Graduate*, who became a household name when she shockingly seduced her daughter's future boyfriend (played by Dustin Hoffman).

As Dr. Ava Cadell, founder of Loveology University, explains it in an interview, "When you get over forty, you want to rekindle your youth, and a good way to do that is through kinky sex. It's sort of an oxymoron. When [women are in their] twenties, we look our best but we have no idea what to do. We're not good communicators. A lot of women lack self-esteem. Once they hit forty, even though they may not be as physically perfect, they have a lot more confidence in speaking their minds."

All genders and ages seem to mix it up and cause intrigue. When Anna Nicole Smith hooked up with a ninety-eight-year-old billionaire, there were questions about the kind of bedroom activity that was really going down with that sixty-three-year age difference. Hugh Hefner, at eighty-two, is still rotating nineteen-year-old girlfriends—in pairs and more. Queen Elizabeth I played with the Earl of Essex's family jewels—she was fifty-three and he was twenty-six. Add the classic novel by Vladimir Nabokov, *Lolita*, where a middle-aged man carries on an obsessive relationship with a precocious twelve-year-old girl.

The list goes on and on in Hollywood: Ralph Fiennes and Francesca Annis, a nineteen-year age difference; Woody Allen and Soon-Yi Previn, thirty-four years (oh, Soon-Yi also happens to be the adopted daughter of his ex-girlfriend—although not yet his ex when they met—Mia Farrow); Charlie Chaplin and Oona O'Neill, thirty-six years; Frank Sinatra and Mia Farrow, thirty-nine years; Tony Randall (who, at seventy-seven, fathered his first child) and Heather Harlan, fifty-one years. Joan Collins married a few younger cubs, one of whom was thirty years her junior.

And although he's not a celebrity, he's worth noting: a Somali man, Ahmed Muhamed Dore, was 112 when he married seventeen-year-old Safia. According to him, it was consensual.

Sex at age ninety is like trying to shoot pool with a rope.

—GEORGE BURNS

COUGAR CRUISE

Carnival Cruise Lines decided to nix the concept of a world's first-ever International Cougar Cruise on their Carnival Elation, despite the excessively high demand for it. So the organizers of the themed cruise went elsewhere, to the Royal Caribbean Mariner of the Seas, and now the popular cruise is hitting the Caribbean seas where cougars and cubs flirt and frolic. The attendants are mixed in with other cruise attendees and given bracelets to distinguish themselves as the cougar and the "prey." One young buck brought his own mother on the second annual cruise. Perhaps she thought it was a good time to prey on some young meat as well.

OH, MRS. ROBINSON . . .

In Northern Ireland, the appropriately named Iris Robinson, at the age of sixty, had an affair with a nineteen-year-old. Not only was she sleeping with him, but she was also helping him financially. She was a member of the British cabinet, though she eventually resigned after their relationship was found out (and attempted suicide). Even worse was the fact that her husband of more than forty years was the first minister in the Northern Ireland Assembly, and they had three children together.

AGEISM

Sometimes age really does matter. Take the nineteen-year-old German who refused to sleep with a grandfather who had wined and dined her all night, only because he was too old. The "old" man, Rolf Eden, seventy-seven, famous in Germany for opening the first disco, being a playboy and making striptease popular, sued for ageism in 2007. As he told the German tabloid *Bild Zeitung*, "After all, there are laws against discrimination."

Working Sex

During the 2008 recession, many women turned to sex to pay the bills. Whether it's phone sex, dominatrix work or selling sex toys at a bachelorette party, women are not only feeling more confident about their sexuality; they're making a buck off of it too. And why not? A 2009 OnePoll survey found that men spent more than $5 billion on strippers, adult sites, phone sex and prostitutes in that recession year.

As always, there are mothers out there who turn to prostitution to make ends meet, using it as a survival mechanism to provide for their kids. With divorce rates skyrocketing and the economy slumping, it's no wonder that more women are turning to these professions.

When a man talks dirty to a woman, it's sexual harassment. When a woman talks dirty to a man, it's $3.95 a minute.   —UNKNOWN

One job that seems accessible to mothers is just a phone call away: phone sex. It's turning into a way for mothers to work from home and not have to spend money on a babysitter. While the baby naps with a lullaby playing, Mama makes gargling noises to a man in South Carolina and pretends his testicles are in her mouth.

Another example of women getting a bang for their buck out of a (kinky) situation is Mollena Williams. She spends her days connecting alternative-sex people with other . . . alternative-sex people. And her job's no joke: she's making a full salary plus benefits. Her title is "executive pervert," and she works for websites such as Bondage.com and Alt.com. She's an expert in bondage and discipline/dominance and submission/sadism and masochism (BDSM) a subject she not only indulges in but also lectures on. With kink going mainstream, her business is booming, with hundreds of people signing up daily to find other like-minded partners. According to a 2009 *Huffington Post* article, Mollena's definition of kinky sex is "sex that's pursued with maximum pleasure in mind, as opposed to, say, procreation." She's also earning more titles—she was Miss San Francisco Leather 2009 and International Miss Leather 2010.

The Feng Shui of Sex

Ariel Joseph Towne is the "feng shui guy." He works with clients with different needs ranging from finances to health. When it comes to a healthy sex life, he'll tell you how to spice up your bedroom to make it sexy by eliminating junk and designing furniture juxtaposition. A couple of his suggestions: don't have a picture of Grandma staring at you in bed; make sure you have enough room for another person (for example: is your bed against a wall, with only one side accessible? Yeah? Then move it!); make sure your sex toys are within an arm's reach (interrupting passion to go find the vibrator in a messy closet kills the mood); add passion colors wherever you can: reds, golds, oranges, pinks; and basically get rid of anything that's a distraction.

"If you want to be shackled to your bed," Towne says, "you may want a four-poster, you might want to have places where you can wrap scarves around your wrists near where your headboard is. And make sure it is made of wood."

In a nutshell: Make the bedroom a place only for *rest* and *play*. And know what you want, even before you invite someone into your bedroom. As Towne explains, "You have to be a solid one before you can be a two . . . and beyond." Towne suggests doing things in pairs, especially if that is what you are into. Odd numbers are more "active" so if you're into that, get that threesome vibe going by surrounding yourself in threes: three dripping candles, three passionate roses, three shapes of vibrators . . .

Two

THE BASICS
OF KINK

Kinky means all sorts of different things to all sorts of different people. But one thing is clear: if you're going to go beyond the missionary, you have to trust your partner. You have to trust them when you're locked up in handcuffs and the key is nowhere in sight. You have to trust them as you're whipped and your head is covered with a gas mask. You have to trust them to believe you when you say, "That's enough Saran Wrap for me." And they, in turn, have to trust you. No matter what you do behind closed bedroom doors, whether it be missionary with a blanket between you or the wheelbarrow position, trust is what makes kinky evolve and is what strengthens relationships inside and outside of the bedroom. If you can't trust your partner, your sex will never progress.

Safe, sane and consensual (SSC) is the motto for most kinky sex players. And when you step things up a notch from just the plain ol' missionary position, it's a good motto to have. Dr. Ava Cadell of the Loveology University talks about boundaries and how important it is to discuss one's sexual and emotional boundaries so that they don't get overstepped. "Communicating our wants, needs, desires and fears is the most difficult thing for us," she says. "Because nobody's ever taught us how to say, 'I want you to pee on me in the shower.' So there's a fear of ridicule, rejection and judgment."

Discovering yourself, your turn-ons and what really makes you tick is enormously important. However, with the popularization of kinky sex, sometimes what's important gets lost in what we think we're supposed to feel. Dr. Cadell explains that some of her clients "cannot satisfy their quench for bigger, better orgasms. And then we really have to look at the big issue there. Why can't a kiss just be an incredible kiss? Why do they need to always watch porn or always be in control when they have sex?" Porn star and Playboy Radio host Nikki Hunter cautions as well: "This is the slippery slope when it comes to kinks and fetishes . . . It's all about what's taboo in your mind. When you see it done, you're like, okay, I went there, what's the next hurdle?" Hunter goes on to explain that sometimes people just want to keep pushing their limits, sometimes to the point of doing illegal activities. She advises, "You have to be very, very careful in exploring your own kinks and being able to find a stopping point, something that satisfies you, and stick with it."

So getting down to the basics of kink is more an exploration of a person's sexual threshold. There's a figurative line that a woman or man draws in the sand that represents the caution *I dare my partner to make me cross this line.* Some people's thresholds are farther down the proverbial beach than others. But the basics of kinkiness all have the same root: the discovery of a situation that is surprisingly sexually gratifying or satisfying or passionate when all along you never knew it could be this good. So let's kick things up a notch and find out how people are quenching their sexual desires.

Going Beyond the Missionary

Sexy is using a feather; kinky is using the whole chicken.

—UNKNOWN

When a woman decides to get on top for the first time, something changes in her and, possibly, in the man beneath her. Their repertoire of standard sex practices changes. When a woman suddenly turns and gets down on her hands and knees for the first time, with her man staring down her backside instead of her chest, something once again changes in them. First cowgirl, then doggy-style, then reverse doggy-style, then wheelbarrow, then anal penetration, then the Flying Lotus, and before you know it, you're hanging from the rafters dressed in a pink latex suit while your wife sucks on your toes. Where does kinkiness begin? Where does it end? Toys are introduced, new orifices are discovered and then friends, strangers and family members are brought into the fray. The next morning may bring shame, laughs or round two. Just what is it about kinkiness that appears to bring out our most carnal and intimate needs?

In 2005, the international condom manufacturer Durex conducted a study showing that 20 percent of adults worldwide were into some type of kinky sex. No doubt that number is higher today. What that means and how risqué the act is, is open to interpretation. But what it most definitely means is that more bedrooms everywhere are heating up and resembling a Gene Simmons hotel suite.

So why is kinky sex expanding the minds of so many people so quickly? Dr. Cadell explains that as we evolve as human beings "mentally, physically, spiritually, we're becoming more experimental in everything that we do, technology-wise and sexually. We have an insatiable appetite for more, as humans. And unfortunately, we're also extremely self-destructive because it's never enough. So with kinky sex, there has to be a balance; otherwise it won't be satisfying."

People can sometimes go to extremes in how they want to achieve sexual fulfillment. There are even drugs illicit or legal— and some are actually prescribed like Viagra or the "female Viagra" pill Flibanserin—that people take to get their sexual groove on. In a nutshell, while wading the waters of sexual satisfaction, it's important to recognize one's own limitations.

It's been so long since I've had sex, I forget who ties up whom.

—JOAN RIVERS

Fantasies

Most studies show that more people than not fantasize about their sex lives. Whether it's about their own spouse, the next-door neighbor, a coworker or a celebrity, people find themselves dreaming about what it'd be like to get it on with another person—and in unusual ways they'd be way too embarrassed to admit to. A UK psychotherapist, Brett Kahr, surveyed 19,000 Brits in 2007 who acknowledged that they fantasized about a little S&M and even harsh play with their partners. This British Sexual Fantasy Research Project found that 96 percent of men and 90 percent of women have sexual fantasies.

There are various theories for why people have fantasies. "Evolutionary psychologists have suggested that sexual fantasies contribute to the facilitation of sexual arousal, which, in turn, facilitates procreation," says Kahr in an interview with the *London Times*. "Freudian psychotherapists and psychoanalysts, by contrast, have speculated that our fantasies may have developed as a means both of gratifying wishes and of conquering intrusive memories of early traumatic experiences."

A research team from Johns Hopkins and other universities found in a 1999 study that people were able to tolerate pain better—like when you're getting wisdom teeth pulled out—if they fantasized about sex. It's even suggested as an alternative to taking pain medicine.

Master Feenix, who dresses in full Victorian garb while he flogs people in a nightclub, explains that fantasies should be acted out. "Everybody has fantasies and the process of going through and living them out makes larger, more self-actualized people. It empowers us if we do it in a safe way with someone we can trust," he says. He goes on to explain how acting out these fantasies makes people cross a threshold of fear and, in turn, empowers them. As Feenix puts it, "You've accomplished something, you've faced up to fear and conquered it, you've gained acceptance for something you felt you had to hide."

Either way, the toughest part appears to be acting out fantasies with someone who'll go along with it—or not acting out the ones that will scare away loved ones or that are simply illegal. But apparently when one does it, and it goes well, it can lead to a whole new lease on your sex life.

Role-Playing

A lot of people are into role-playing. While it's a fun way to act out a scenario with someone you're with, it's really about creating a fantasy world you'd *like* to be in. There are priest and nun role-playing ("Get on your knees!"), delivery-boy fantasies ("Brought you some pie, ma'am"), policemen fantasies ("Stick 'em up and let me slide it in"), and so on. The list is endless.

A Different Card Game

Dr. Cadell gives the following advice when it comes to role-playing: "Take baby steps. Role-playing is a great way to take baby steps and to explore what turns you on and what turns your partner on." And she offers a fun way to enhance this activity—she has created a deck of cards, called Role Playing Fantasy cards. On one side of a card there's a picture of a sexy "character" and on the other there are instructions on suggested props and how to role-play that character. They are gender appropriate and there's no way to lose at this game, as they are sure to create an intriguing evening spent at home!

Flagellation

I think there are a lot of things in regular life that can be highly erotic that don't end in a sexual act . . . So it's not surprising . . . that you can connect through someone erotically while you have them naked and bound to a cross and you're gently flogging their flesh and bringing the level up slowly until you're really stimulating them with pain.

—GODDESS SOMA

From criminals and naughty children to vixens and shameless CEOs, *paddling* is humanity's pastime. Our societies have been paddling one another as a type of corporal punishment for thousands of years. Now, paddling's been taken up in the bedroom and beyond, with countless types of sculls available to play with, from a rolled-up magazine, a simple ruler or an actual paddle. New York City's S&M club Paddles is one of the oldest clubs of its kind in Manhattan (some say in the United States). Upon entering, there's no way to miss the table consisting of every possible kind of paddle out there: studded, balled, furry, spiked, laced, you name it. You can take your pick and have the Master or Mistress at hand dish out whatever you can take.

Flogging was used back in prehistory all the way from the Roman Empire to the French Revolution to the British Navy to today's prisons and schools around the world. It is still a form of punishment in some Islamic and Asian countries. Sticks, whips and rods were used to beat a person on the back. With all the education that comes hand in hand with BDSM today, participants know which areas of the body (like the kidneys) to avoid in order not to cause permanent damage. Today, floggers are made out of anything from feathers to horsehair to elk hide, and designed into styles like cat-o'-nine-tails.

Whips are designed in a variety of ways, often made of bull hide or just a birch. *Canes* are often made of rattan, and are not the canes used for walking sticks (those are thicker and more rigid). Usually in the form of feathers, *ticklers* are a great way to segue your lover into a little rougher play, especially if they have a knismolagnia (or tickling) fetish.

> *You don't appreciate a lot of stuff in school until you get older. Little things like being spanked every day by a middle-aged woman: Stuff you pay good money for in later life.* —EMO PHILIPS

The Victorian era put *spanking* on the kinky map. It was written about and even illustrated, then secretly read and savored by conservatives of that time. In the 1980s, spanking magazines were popular, both for men and women. The spanking bench (or horse) looks a bit like a sawhorse, and the submissive is tied down or handcuffed to it so that the Dominant can spank the crap out of him or her.

Many clients enter dungeons or nightclubs in order to get some corporal punishment, to be tied up and then caned, spanked or flogged. Master Feenix works at the Los Angeles club Bar Sinister on the weekends (his day job is working with a porn production company). He will "play" with people who want him to dominate them. "One of the most rewarding aspects is being a safe space for people to experience their fantasy about being dominated. That's a really wonderful thing for me," he says. These fantasies in the club include being tied up and flogged, whipped or lightly spanked. It can be a huge turn-on, as Feenix explains. "I've had women orgasm with me playing with them in front of everyone in the nightclub." But at the same time, Feenix doesn't find what he does as being necessarily sexual. "I look at it as energetic. Just as hunger creates a drive in you, sexuality creates a hunger as well. And that hunger can be satisfied or addressed in ways that don't actually involve genital stimulation and orgasm."

Plus, there have been plenty of personalities who have admitted to a little ass-whopping. Cindy Margolis, former *Playboy* pinup and once the "most downloaded woman," talked about how her favorite bedroom fun is "a good vibrator and a paddle that I give to my man." And the king of radio, Howard Stern, has his own paddling machine in his studio called the "Robospanker," where he's seen many a lass be spanked.

Once Bitten, Twice as Confident

With the mania over vampires, from *Twilight* to *True Blood*, biting is—and has always been—in. Of course, biting is not something everyone can sink their teeth into. And following in Marv Albert's footsteps, where the famous sportscaster apologized in court for biting a woman numerous times on her back, is not the way to go.

But many love to bite. A nibble here or there has been known to spice up more than one person's sex life. It's the remnants of our reptilian brains that causes us to instinctually bite. If you're in Africa and you whack a lion on the ass, he's going to bite you. If you've ever had children, you know when they're infants, they have the tendency to bite you for no reason other than because it feels right. When two lovers are folded into sexual expression, it's

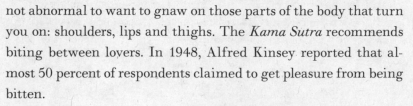

Paralyzing Hickey

One New Zealand woman came to the hospital unable to move her arm because of a hickey. The hickey was so deep that it released a small blood clot in a nearby artery, which caused a minor stroke, paralyzing her temporarily.

not abnormal to want to gnaw on those parts of the body that turn you on: shoulders, lips and thighs. The *Kama Sutra* recommends biting between lovers. In 1948, Alfred Kinsey reported that almost 50 percent of respondents claimed to get pleasure from being bitten.

Supposedly, Marilyn Monroe liked to bite her lover's lips until they bled. And Napoleon Bonaparte was bitten while having sex with Josephine on their wedding night—but not by her; by their dog, who either thought Napoleon was attacking his new wife or was just mad about having to share his bed with another person.

Sexting

Sexting is sending sex messages, usually in the form of photos of body parts and nudity, to another person's cell phone. It's become popular but it's also gotten people into trouble. It was this kind of hard evidence that brought down golfer Tiger Woods. Vikings' quarterback Brett Favre allegedly sent "cock shots" to *Daily Line*

The F— List

One student at Duke University, Karen Owen, had her "fuck list" spiral out of control into cyberspace after she put together a "thesis" on all the guys she had screwed called "An Education Beyond the Classroom: Excelling in the Realm of Horizontal Academics." And it wasn't just a list; it was a PowerPoint presentation, complete with names and photos, details and scores on their sex, their dirty sex talk, their sexting abilities and their overall sexual abilities. The clincher was that most of these guys were the "studs" on campus, such as lacrosse players. Apparently, Owen had written this as a joke for a few friends, who then sent it to their friends, who sent it on to other friends, and on and on till even NBC's *Today* show was talking about it.

reporter Jenn Sterger and got busted. And Detroit mayor Kwame Kilpatrick was caught sexting more than 14,000 texts to his chief of staff—on a taxpayer-supplied phone.

Group Sex

I believe that sex is a beautiful thing between two people. Between five, it's fantastic.
　　　　　　　　　　　　　　　　　　—WOODY ALLEN

The more the merrier. Group sex is a thousands-years-old practice. The Hindus were into it, creating Tantric and *Kama Sutra* ceremonies with groups of people coupling together, conveying a sacred, beautiful event. However, group sex—or orgies—is an activity that can veer toward dangerous areas with strangers coming in and out from all directions. And it can be especially threatening to a relationship if everything isn't discussed beforehand and boundaries aren't agreed upon; rules must be crystal clear. Even then, people's emotions normally trump logic and feelings, and relationships can be injured.

A simple variation of group sex is the threesome, where a third person is added into the mix. As Larry Flynt said, "One of the common fantasies of men and some women is to have three in their bed . . . To many people, that's kinky. The people I know, that's not kinky. That's just having great sex."

Par Three

Hugh Hefner isn't the only one parading around with multiple girlfriends. Charlie Sheen made headline news in early 2011 when he revealed that he lived and slept with two "goddesses." One was a bikini model and the other was a porn star. The two goddesses claimed to take care of his kids and lead a "normal life" when the cameras weren't around.

And Tiger Woods apparently paid $4,000 for a night of threesome sex that included "porn queen" Devon James, according to James herself. Michelle Braun also confirmed that the golfer was into having a lot of extra girls in bed with him.

Swinging

Swinging's all about what it sounds like—swinging from one partner to the next, or doing them in groups. Some say it strengthens marriages since everything's out in the open and participants can act on their sexual urges. It's something they can do as a couple, where both can be totally involved in it and then go home together fulfilled. There's no itching to try something new, no worries about hiding an infidelity. From wife-swapping centuries ago to key parties, swinging has its place in society, regardless of it being a very personal and acquired taste.

Archaeologist Timothy Taylor from the University of Bradford argues that monogamy came about in society only when hunter-gatherer societies became more stable, living in houses and taking up agriculture, and therefore having more regulated roles for men

Cruisin'

Swingers have departed from key parties and Craigslist to embark on special swingers' cruises. Companies such as YOLO Cruises have used liners such as Carnival to take swinging to the waters. The first time it took place was in 2009 in the Caribbean. Now more ships have set sail for swingers, where people trot the boats naked, have sex in designated areas with whomever they want and partake in the special themed lifestyle parties (where, yes, you can be nude).

and women. Jumping ahead thousands of years, the United States thought they were the "inventors" of swinging. But since the 1700s, the French have been trading off wives, husbands and partners to one another. Statistics are hard to find on how many swingers are out there, but the most popular dating website for the activity, AdultFriendFinder.com, has more than 34 million members as of 2010, if that's any indication.

Remember Plato's Retreat in New York City? It was probably the most famous swingers' club for heterosexuals. It got shut down in the mid-eighties when AIDS took center stage. Back in 1969, Paul Mazursky directed the first mainstream movie about swinging, called *Bob & Carol & Ted & Alice*. China even has a website

Swinging for Rights

One arrest in China that made news was of the country's most famous swinger, former professor Ma Yaohai. At age fifty-three, he was imprisoned for what a Chinese court deemed to be "crowd licentiousness." He had been organizing and participating in orgies, with the venue sometimes being his mother's apartment. And he'd troll websites with the username Roaring Virile Fire. But Yaohai is fighting back, demanding privacy laws and saying his sex life is nobody's business but his own. He's appealing the court decision, in a country where pornography is banned. Still, it's progress. According to a 2010 *New York Times* article, "18 Orgies Later, Chinese Swinger Gets Prison Bed," in the 1980s, the owner of a secret swingers' club in China was simply arrested and executed.

called Happy Village that's a chat forum for swingers. And it's a subject that's now in mainstream media, with CBS even having produced a prime-time show in 2008 called *Swingtown*.

Dogging

The term "dogging" is British slang for orgies in a semipublic place, like a parked car or in a park. But it's become more than that, especially in England. People connect online, decide on a location, go in various cars and swap partners in the numerous vehicles, and there are plenty of people who watch and possibly join in themselves. It's a perfect storm of exhibitionism, the Internet, sex and lots of horny people. It was reported in a 2003 survey by Richard Byrne, a lecturer at Harper Adams University College in the UK, that 60 percent of UK parks hold "dogging" meet-ups.

Polyamory

Swingers have sex. Polys have conversations.
—A JOKE THAT ATTEMPTS TO EXPLAIN POLYAMORY

In America (as well as other countries, such as New Zealand), polyamory (openly loving more than one person with the consent of everyone involved—otherwise known as "ethical non-monogamy") is on the rise. According to the TLC program *Strange Sex* there are half a million people in the United States in polyamorous relationships. And those are only the ones who admit to it. More and more people are coming out of the woodwork, opening up about their private lives. A lot of this is said to be due to the Internet. But even though the idea of multiple partners is as old as human history, Yale theologian John Humphrey Noyes in 1848 founded a commune in upstate New York that spoke of polyamory. And then the free love days of the 1960s and '70s made it more popular. It wasn't until the 1990s that "polyamory" was put into the dictionaries.

Basically, here's how it usually goes: "Arnold" and "Alice" are living together as a couple. Then Alice finds "Bruce," with whom she wants to be in a relationship. After introducing Bruce to Arnold and getting Arnold's approval, Alice invites Bruce to live with them. Then Arnold falls for "Bonnie," and the same introduction/approval happens. Then Bonnie says she's involved with Chuck and reveals that he too wants to live there. Somehow, this type of open relationship works for some people. They don't consider any of it cheating since they are all open about what they are doing, making sure that no one is hurt or jealous (although that can happen). It's not just sex; it's living life together, paying the bills and mortgage, dealing with kids and other kinks that life brings. Although naturally group sex can find its way into the bedroom, there are plenty of relationships that remain one-on-one when it comes to sex.

The way Miss Nikki Nefarious, who has a polyamorous relationship with her husband, who lives on the other side of the country, explains it is, "There's open communication and honesty so there's no real cheating that happens. Everyone knows what's going on. Most times there's pre-approval that's needed and yes, there's sex outside of marriage, but if it's within my marriage, it's not outside of my marriage. This is within what we do together." She has a boyfriend in Los Angeles and is openly bisexual. Meanwhile, her husband in North Carolina has a girlfriend about whom Miss Nikki says, "I love her to death, she's amazing. She's like my sister that I would not have met or gotten close to had it not been for this arrangement. I'm really lucky."

A 2009 *Newsweek* article, "Only You. And You. And You," stated that there are more than half a million *open* polyamorous families in the United States. Which means there are plenty more than that who are not so open about their activities.

The Poly Life

Actress Tilda Swinton has an intriguing arrangement from what the press can tell. She lives in Scotland with her twins' father, John Byrne, with whom she's been together for years. But she also carries on a relationship with a New Zealand painter, Sandro Dopp, who's twenty years her junior. She's never been married, but she's always had at least one of these guys by her side: Sandro is usually the one who travels with her, while John stays at home. Sandro does stay in the same house with them sometimes, but there's no definitive answer on who's sleeping in which bed.

Anal Sex

Anal sex (or sodomy) is an act that can be found throughout history. Often considered a sin, anal sex was punishable by death in many cultures. The Bible's Sodom and Gomorrah made the term famous. God wasn't too happy about homosexuality in these two cities, and so destroyed them. Today, it is still illegal to have anal sex in some countries and even some US states.

The anus has more nerve endings than any other part of the body, so it can cause major pleasure (and pain). Whether it's a penis, a fist or any other device you desire, there's one main word of advice while engaging in anal: use lots of lube. (But don't use numbing creams. If there's pain, something's wrong—and you should be able to feel it and see your physician right away.)

There's a misconception that anal sex is a homosexual activity. It can be, but it's definitely a heterosexual one as well, with plenty

Tainted Lovin'

Porn star Jenna Jameson wrote in her 2004 autobiography, *How to Make Love Like a Porn Star: A Cautionary Tale*, that when it came to anal sex, "This is almost embarrassing for a porn star to admit, but I've only given that up to three men, all of whom I really loved. Doing it on camera would be compromising myself."

of couples enjoying it on a regular basis. The 2010 national sex survey that was published in the *Journal of Sexual Medicine* found that 40 percent of women between the ages of eighteen and twenty-four had tried anal sex, up from 24 percent in a 1992 survey. And back in 2005, the Centers for Disease Control's National Survey of Family Growth found that 38.2 percent of men and 32.6 percent of women in their twenties and thirties were getting into this back-end type of delivery.

Solo Suck

If I really got my ribs removed, I would have been busy sucking my own dick on The Wonder Years *instead of chasing Winnie Cooper. Besides, I wouldn't have sucked other people's dicks onstage, either. I would have been sucking my own. Plus, who really has time to be killing puppies when you can be sucking your own dick? I think I'm gonna call the surgeon in the morning.* —MARILYN MANSON

America's Al Eingang is a famous solo sucker, literally making a living off of it. He is able to give himself constant blow jobs at any time of day or night. His tips for men to be able to perform auto-fellatio? Lots of stretching and yoga. He claims that no matter the size of the penis, solo sucking is a sport every man can enjoy. Alfred Kinsey differed on that, having stated that less than 1 percent of men can even connect with their penis to consider this act. And another study by William Guy, MA, and Michael H. P. Finn, PhD, in 1954 suggested that only two or three out of a thousand men are big enough to actually perform the act.

Yet this is a practice that has history, with ancient hieroglyphics and paintings depicting men getting off on their own, and references to this in many texts dealing with Egyptian religion. Today, porn rarely shows the act, but there have been some, most notably by the "Hedgehog" Ron Jeremy (before he put on weight).

Autocunnilingus is the act of a woman going down on herself. She'd probably have to be a contortionist to get it done and there's very little information out there as to whether anyone has succeeded.

Kinky Bible Study

Miss Nikki Nefarious is also a devout Christian, and grew up believing in God. While she doesn't attend church today, she still prays every day and reads the Bible. Now she's about to start hosting a Bible study class "for 'us' people because most of the people in church, if they knew what I did, they'd drum me right out of church. And that's why I want to do this, and say, God made me, God does not make trash, contrary to what you might think. We're not going to be talking about kinky things. We're going to be talking about us as kinky people, living our kinky lifestyles, being kinky humans who are still good Christians and can still have our connection [with God] . . ." Amen!

BDSM

BDSM stands for "bondage and discipline/dominance and submission/sadism and masochism." While to some people this term conjures up frightening images of people beating the crap out of one another while dressed like rubber horror dolls, more and more people are appreciating this lifestyle and are identifying themselves with one or more of them.

For many BDSMers, their activities are about pushing the psychological and physiological boundaries of a person in order to get the greatest release, sexually and mentally. It seems as if every sense is tapped into and awakened, in order to feel the full effect of what is being done, whether it's flogging or binding. Participants believe that playing in the BDSM world restores balance in their lives, where they search and find what it is they are lacking. They then fulfill that void. For example, a CEO of a large company, who constantly has to make decisions and be in control, lets loose in a dungeon, eagerly being treated and acting like a submissive, gets tied up by a dominatrix and whipped till he can no longer take it. As Miss Nikki explains it: "I always resonated with BDSM because it wasn't about sex; it's more about a mental or emotional release."

When it comes to the pain aspect, which is often mistakenly seen as the core of BDSM, Dr. Paul Federoff of the University of Ottawa in a 2004 *Time* magazine article, "Bondage Unbound," points out that "pain is a means to an end, but not the goal itself." Sometimes, pain doesn't even have to take place; just the mere anticipation of pain is enough to get some people off.

SM vs. S&M

There is a difference between SM and S&M. Basically, "S&M" is the term for those who dabble in kinkiness only occasionally (let's say, kink lite) and aren't serious about it; it's also the term used for all the pop culture associated with this lifestyle (like Madonna's kinky outfits). "SM" is for those who are deeply involved in that world.

According to the *Time* magazine article, there are more than 250 SM organizations in the United States alone. A 1990 Kinsey Institute report said researchers estimated that 5 percent to 10 percent of Americans occasionally engaged in S&M sex. And while kinky people are still the minority, there are organizations, such as the National Coalition for Sexual Freedom, working for BDSM people's rights (their 2008 survey found 38 percent of people who call themselves kinky were harassed for it). There have been court cases where people who consented to BDSM practices later managed to sue for assault—and in court, consent isn't a defense. There's the 1996 case of Oliver Jovanovic, who was convicted of kidnapping and sexually abusing a Columbia undergrad. What was interesting was that his conviction was later overturned because the trial court didn't allow the jury to see the alleged victim's emails, which happened to state all of her S&M fantasies. The charges were then dismissed in a second trial because the victim refused to testify.

Obviously there are plenty of things that people like about this lifestyle. Goddess Soma explains that some of the best things about being in the BSDM world is "the community aspect. A lot of people really take it seriously as a family, a support system . . . I think the level of intimacy that you can achieve is so much higher than a lot of people ever experience in vanilla relationships. For me, it's creative sexual expression and being able to be bizarre and weird (as in, socially unacceptable) and a little bit Fellini-esque at moments."

LET'S BREAK DOWN BDSM

Bondage

This is about tying someone up in order to restrict their movements. Sure, sometimes we'll play with scarves, which won't cause any harm to the skin. Or maybe we'll throw on a pair of handcuffs. But there are others who are specifically trained to do this sort of bondage, learning the technique and art of Japanese rope bondage among others. Some popular areas of the body that get tied up are the breasts, face, penis and feet. But some people are into the whole deal, getting completely mummified by rope, twine or fabric from head to toe.

There are popular bondage artists in the United States, such as Midori and Twisted Monk (who makes his own hemp ropes). Kink. com's founder, Peter Acworth, claims that he had erections when he'd watch cowboy and Indian shows on TV as a boy, where people constantly got tied up. Now he makes movies about bondage. Miss Nikki Nefarious is an award-winning bondage artist who started young, tying up her Barbies and neighborhood boys. "All I know is when I was playing with ropes, it just made me concentrate," she explains. Carol Queen, PhD, staff sexologist at Good Vibrations, explains it in the *Men's Health* article "2,131 Women Confess to Us," saying, "There is a sense of being erotically overwhelmed that comes along with being restrained, and many women find it quite passionate . . . Women are encouraged to understand themselves as objects of desire, and through bondage and restraint, there's an acting out of that."

But rope isn't the only equipment used to bind someone. Other things people use in order to bond someone into the right position are bars, chains, collars, crucifixes, cages, cuffs, encasement, gags, harnesses, hoods, lace, mittens, padlocks, rape racks, shackles and straitjackets. Just to name a few.

Discipline

Part of taking control means disciplining your submissive subject. The submissive loves to be reminded how his or her parents used to discipline them. Or they enjoy the fact that they are for once being disciplined and not the other way around. Whether it's being whipped for doing something bad, kneeling in a corner for hours, verbal humiliation or scrubbing dirty toilet bowls, there is a chemistry with being submissive that charges some people's sexuality.

Dominant

The Dominant will control a submissive who will adhere to them and abide by their every rule. Dominant men are called many things, which include "master," "mister," "sir" and "lord." Dominant women have a variety of titles, including "goddess," "mistress," "domina," "lady," "empress" and "princess." The traditional process is for someone to obtain a mentor and work their way up, earning their titles. But in some of the BDSM communities, there's no particular structure. And yet in worlds like the leather world, there's a very strict regimen of how one becomes a Dominant, or even how one enters that community to begin with.

But going back to the basic power dynamic for a Dominant, there are Dominants who date each other, but usually one has to become submissive to the other. Or there are Dominants who "top" a submissive, which means they may or may not have a power relationship with them but they can dominate. Dominants can "co-top" a submissive during play, which means they dominate a submissive together during, say, a flogging session.

Master Feenix, who works in a nightclub as a Dominant and whips willing participants, has a submissive girlfriend, and he explains their relationship: "I think that's why she was attracted to me and why I was attracted to her. She is a naturally submissive person who was looking for a relationship in which she could ex-

There and Back

A *switch* is someone who can switch back and forth from being a Dominant to a submissive. Not everyone in the BDSM world is capable of doing that.

plore and express her submissive nature. And I'm a dominant man so I am only interested in women who will be submissive to me."

Mistress Nikki Hunter explains that being a Dominant isn't only about control. "Half of it has to deal with sex and power play, but the other half is being a therapist," she explains. "Really, you're drawing on things that are so deep in a person's mind on why they like to be gangbanged or why they like to do strangers or be tied up. It's a huge mental thing."

Submission

A submissive (or "sub" or "bottom," which means they may or may not have a power relationship with the "top") is someone who relinquishes all control to a Dominant.

Even though it doesn't sound politically correct, most submissives turn out to be women, despite what the public usually hears about men going to dominatrixes who take control. In the *Time* magazine article "Bondage Unbound," Dr. Paul Fedoroff of the University of Ottawa spoke about studying sadomasochism and found that out of 1,320 BDSM participants, 79 percent of the women said they were submissive, as opposed to 35 percent of the men.

These submissives are also sometimes called "slaves." They live with their masters and mistresses, obeying their every demand, sometimes on a 24/7 basis, sometimes on a sexual basis, and sometimes just to do the chores—but always consensually. They will endure humiliation and torture for pleasure. Some slaves write up contracts with their Dominants, stating how long they are contractually going to be their slave, whether it's for three months or for life. Master Feenix says he has a servant (he does not like to use the word "slave") who does maintenance work around his home. "I pay her in my attention," he said when asked if the servant gets paid for her work. At the same time, their relationship is strictly platonic.

Goddess Soma's slave, "Boy," is a woman-to-man transgender who lives with her 24/7. As Soma explains, "We always stay in character. There are levels of protocol, when we're more casual with each other at certain times, and times when he's under really strict instructions on how he holds his body and sits. But we always call each other 'goddess' and 'boy.' He always serves me." Soma also has a boyfriend who lives with her when he's not traveling, and is submissive to her but "not as far as Boy." But she trusts that her boyfriend will be submissive and faithful to her at all times. Meanwhile, Soma does have other sex partners, except they are female (her boyfriend is her only male sex partner); she is sometimes intimate with Boy, who is also intimate with one of Soma's girlfriends. As Master Feenix jokes about all the relationships in general, "You really need a flowchart."

There are those who believe that, contrary to what people might

The Drill

In the movie *Little Shop of Horrors*, the character played by Jack Nicholson in 1960, and then by Bill Murray in 1986, goes to the dentist not because he needs work done but because he needs a fix for his pain fetish.

think, the submissives are the ones in control of the relationship—because they can end it at any time they desire, and their Dominant has to respect that. Master Feenix explains that "all of the power comes from the submissive. All of the control comes from the Dominant. [These are] power-exchange roles. The submissive is giving up their power of self-direction to the control of the Dominant. But that is a decision that can be revoked at any time. My servant saying, 'I accept you as my sir' . . . All of that comes from the submissive's voluntary pledge to submit." But they can get up one morning and say good-bye and end it right there and then.

Sadism

This is about inflicting pain on someone, or just watching pain being inflicted on someone—and enjoying it.

Donatien Alphonse François, Comte de Sade (1740–1814), or the Marquis de Sade as he's better known, was the father of sadism. He was the writer of many works that involved hard-core porn, novels such as *The 120 Days of Sodom*, *Juliette* and *Justine*. His mention of power-play sex toys, such as whips, nipple clamps and restraints, made them popular.

But sadism is thought to have been invented even earlier. The *Kama Sutra*, written in the third or fourth century, referred to sexual spankings and other variations of S&M practices. In AD 1100, medieval torture devices were used in a sexual manner. But around the time of the Marquis de Sade, brothels in Europe were specializing in S&M, beating the crap out of submissive clients, such as members of political parties and other powerful figures.

Masochism

Masochism is the mind-set of someone who enjoys receiving pain. These people like to suffer, and often will want to suffer as much as possible.

In 1870, author Leopold von Sacher-Masoch wrote the novel *Venus in Furs*, which spoke about male submission to a woman. From his name came the word "masochism."

Slavercise

New York City is home to plenty of BDSM. But here's an innovative take on becoming someone's slave: there are "slavercise" classes now available, which are a form of workout involving S&M. For $150 an hour (private couple session) or $20 an hour (class), a dominatrix in leather garb, high heels and a riding crop literally whips you into shape and will "beat the fat out of your body" (a workout video is available as well, although it may not have the same effects).

One mistress who runs these types of classes is Mistress Victoria (Holly DeRito), who has a journalism degree but realized there was a lot more money in the S&M world. She gets people in shape while kicking their asses. She makes her students oink if they're not squatting right. She rides a student like a horse when they forget their leg stretches. And she has men wear pink tutus if they screw up during the workout. But no fear: true to BDSM form, there are safe words that the instructor will abide by. And as stated on the website, Slavercise. com, cross-dressing and fetish attire is welcome but not mandatory.

There are plenty of other aspects to the BDSM world. Here are a few more:

The lifestyle: Usually refers to people in one niche community, like the leather community, where they embrace all aspects of the lifestyle.

Lifestyler: This is someone who is not necessarily involved in the S&M scene, but who accepts their Dominant or submissive roles and their relationship as a way of life inside their own home. They don't live this life 24/7 and have outside routines that have nothing to do with S&M.

Power exchange: This is the official transfer of power when the submissive gives in to the Dominant, and in exchange, the Dominant empowers the submissive.

Play: The overall term for people having a BDSM interaction. There are erotic undertones to it but it isn't necessarily sexual. Some "play" is sexy but not sex: flogging, bondage, tease and denial (getting someone worked up but refusing to allow them sexual satisfaction).

Goddess Soma explains that outside of her boyfriend, girlfriends and slave, she also has "play" partners, people she plays with but doesn't own. By that she means, "I don't have control on what they do in their outside life, only what we would do within a play scene."

Energy play is another variation of play that is more intense, where it's all about feeling your own energy together with someone else's. As Miss Nikki Nefarious says, "If you're really lucky, you can find a partner who's into energy play, and that's the closest thing to actually connecting on that level you can possibly get."

Head play is basically all about messing with one's mind, manipulating the situation so that the submissive/bottom is anticipating more in terms of punishment or whatever else provokes them. A total "mind-fuck."

And *edge play* is about those who are more hard-core or advanced. Their style of play is on the periphery of what's "safe."

Scene: It's part of "play," a limited-time activity in S&M, such as getting tied up and whipped, with an understood beginning and ending.

Session: Most Dominants who are professional have time with their clients that they refer to as a "session." It may or may not refer to actual sex; it's more about the S&M activity.

Negotiation: Partners decide together what will happen once they start their relationship—whether it's for a scene or for their life together—so that they both know where they stand, what they are allowed to do and how far they can go. Everything is negotiated up front so that no one is hurt in the long run.

Safe word: This is the word that literally gets you out of a "bind." It's a word that is agreed upon before any BDSM relationship takes place, no matter how short the relationship is. And a safe word isn't "no" or "yes." It can be "red" for stop or "green" for carry on. Or any other word that you won't forget—be creative!

Kinky Flicks

I think S&M in the movie is in a lot of ways a metaphor for the complications in life, the fact that there is both light and dark in every relationship and in every person. And that pain helps to define what pleasure is. —MAGGIE GYLLENHAAL

There are plenty of movies with kinky scenes in them, from mainstream to documentary to indie. *Belle de Jour, The Night Porter, 9½ Weeks, Crash, Blue Velvet, Secretary* and *The Notorious Bettie Page* all have kinky scenes, stories and/or subplots. *Indie Sex* is a comprehensive and fun documentary of all things sexy in the movies over time, with a section devoted to "extremes." *Kinsey* was a great overview about the most famous sexologist. There are also films that are completely focused on the kinky world. There's even a film festival devoted to this subject, called the CineKink Film Festival, held annually in New York City.

Another film worth noting is the cult classic *The Story of O*, based on the 1954 French novel by Pauline Reage. The story is about a submissive woman entering the world of BDSM. This film and book inspired many more TV shows, films, documentaries, songs and comic books.

In *BDSM: It's Not What You Think! Kinksters Confront Stigma and Stereotype*, director Erin Palmquist takes a look at some of the rumors surrounding BDSM and tries to squash them by getting a more honest take on what living this lifestyle means. In her thirty-minute documentary, Palmquist gives viewers a peek inside the world of people who are into BDSM, why it's important for people to be educated about it and how to do it in a safe way.

In *Liberty in Restraint* (2005), director Michael Ney gives an in-depth look into the BDSM scene in Sydney, Australia, through the world of fetish photographer Noel Graydon. It also examines how the fetish world is becoming more mainstream. For someone new to the scene, it describes the appeal of hard-core bondage, even if there are some moments that may be difficult to watch. However, the beautiful cinematography and rope artistry will ease whatever misgivings you may have. "Queen of Kink" artist and sexologist Annie Sprinkle comments that the film is "simply the best documentary on BDSM, and the people that practice and enjoy it, that I've ever seen."

Three

A HISTORICAL
GUIDE TO
DEBAUCHERY

umans have always had three basic needs: food, air and sex. From the day that people could communicate, sex has been written about more than any other subject. Ancient dildos have been dug up on anthropological sites. Our prehistoric ancestors had sex lives similar to bonobo chimps, promiscuous great apes that do not commit to one partner. According to cave paintings, cave women were a sexual bunch, inviting sex by fire-light next to mammoth bones. And according to some sexperts like Dr. Ruth Westheimer, the Bible is the best sex manual and God is the ultimate sex therapist. Throughout history, sex has been front and center. And why not? If not for sex, I would not be typing these words. That's not to say my parents conceived me while one of them was bound and gagged. But not only are we humans sexual beings; we are also explorative beings always searching for the unknown. So with sex comes the exploration of what sex could, can and has become.

I think it is funny that we were freer about sexuality in the fourth century BC. It is a little disconcerting. —ANGELINA JOLIE

Sex Has Always Been Fun

Today, there is scientific evidence to suggest that Stone Age citizens weren't having sex strictly to procreate as originally thought. It's now believed that Neanderthals were tying one another up, engaging in orgies, using sex toys and even making pornographic figurines. This goes against the classic theory that *Homo sapiens* were preprogrammed for monogamy. In reality, monogamy started when hunter-gatherer cultures began to settle, after our minds evolved into consciences that could differentiate between right and wrong. Men's and women's roles in society were changing. The more we planted and sowed and invented and law-enforced and praised symbolic and spiritual values, the more we became prudish squares. Or, put another way, we developed sexual morals.

Masturbation

The good thing about masturbation is that you don't have to get dressed up for it. —TRUMAN CAPOTE

Let's start by setting our way-back machines and examining the way we've all spanked the monkey at one time or another. Some see masturbation as a healthy, invigorating and beautiful thing. To others, wanking is a dark, evil and wasteful event. In many religions, sex is considered appropriate only for making babies. The Bible is opposed to masturbation. However, the ancient Taos believed that self-gratification was a good thing, and that the act could help in achieving immortality. That left much of the growing and impressionable public with the question: "To flog the dolphin or not to flog the dolphin?"

We have reason to believe that man first walked upright to free his hands for masturbation. —LILY TOMLIN

A QUICK LOOK BACK AT MASTURBATION

The island of Malta has a temple site called Hagar Qim where a rare fourth-century BC figurine depicts a woman masturbating. Figurines showing male masturbation were much more common, with depictions even found back in the Neolithic period in Greece, where masturbation was considered natural. Ancient Egyptians believed that their god Amun masturbated and his seed created civilization in general, and that the Nile River's water behavior was in sync with his masturbation cycles.

After the sixteenth century, rumors on the side effects of masturbation became grave and serious warnings, since it was thought that pleasuring oneself could make you deaf, mute and dumb, possibly even epileptic and mentally retarded. People were chastised for their lack of self-control and made to feel like savage barbarians.

In the nineteenth century, there were "cures" for those who masturbated. This was especially true in the Victorian era, with the advent of men's pants made especially tight so they couldn't touch themselves, penis wraps made of spikes, and corsets made of leather and steel to prevent women from groping themselves. No amount of Vaseline would make that a smooth ride.

The Kinsey Reports were a scientific study on human sexual behavior by the man considered to be the father of sexology, Dr. Alfred Kinsey. They came out in the form of two books, *Sexual Behavior in the Human Male* (1948) and *Sexual Behavior in the Human Female* (1953), shocking, offending and relieving many people when it revealed that masturbation wasn't such a bad thing after all. (The report revealed that 92 percent of males and 62 percent of women admitted to masturbating, with it being the most important "sexual outlet" for single females.) Sigmund Freud gave the study vast amounts of merit when he agreed with the results. Then in 1971, Martin Goldstein, Erwin J. Haeberle and Will McBride, authors of *The Sex Book: A Modern Pictorial Encyclopedia*, announced after a research project that masturbating was the most common form of sex by humans.

A 2010 sex survey by the University of Indiana, the largest of its kind since a 1994 nationwide study, showed that people don't view pleasing oneself as a taboo anymore. Dr. Ava Cadell of the Loveology University concurs with this in an interview. "Masturbation is good for your health. Whether you're single or in a relationship, both single or mutual masturbation is fantastic. To me, it's about self-love. I give the prescription of masturbation to all my clients, so it's very important." More people are seeing masturbation as a natural act that shouldn't be ridiculed or deemed a "sin." Again, we're reminded that we share 98.4 percent of our DNA with bonobo chimpanzees, the same chimps that have always masturbated. It's all the same whether you tug it in trees, next to a termite mound or in your mom's basement.

MASTURBATION AROUND THE WORLD

In India, women have called a sex consultant, Dr. Shirish Malde, desperately seeking answers on how to get off on their own—but without breaking their hymens. A 2001 *Marie Claire* study showed 70 percent of Peruvian men admitted to masturbating—but in that same study, not a single woman would admit to it. However, close by in Colombia, 79 percent of women fessed up that they got a little touchy-feely with themselves. In Holland, masturbating is considered so normal that a glossy woman's magazine even offered a free electric vibrator called Tarzan with a subscription, knowing it's probably the best way to gain new subscribers. The magician Penn Jillette (of Penn & Teller) invented the "hydrotherapeutic stimulator," which put a new spin on taking a bath: it's basically a bathtub/hot tub with water streams shooting in all the right places so a woman can really get clean—and off. And there are mastur-bating contests, such as the Masturbate-A-Thon held by the Center for Sex and Culture in San Francisco, where the 2009 champion, Masanobu Sato, held out for nine hours and thirty-three minutes before blowing his (loaded) load.

However you decide to roll, Woody Allen may have put it best: "Don't knock masturbation. It's sex with someone that I love."

The Manuals

Love and sex manuals are a dime a dozen these days, with every-one wanting to get their two cents in, and people wanting to spend more than two cents to find out how to become the best lover possible.

These manuals have been around since mankind started carv-ing shapes into stones. The reason is that humans have never solely relied on their instincts to figure out how to turn someone on—or themselves. We believed there was always someone else who knew more about sex, whether that was true or not.

Authored by the Roman poet Ovid, *The Art of Love* is one of the earliest sex manuals known to exist, written sometime between 1 BC and AD 1. It's a poem spanning three books, where Ovid writes to Roman men about how to locate women in Rome, how to make them love you and how to make sure another guy doesn't take them away.

Most any average Joe can tell you they've heard of the ultimate love book, the *Kama Sutra*. Written around the third or fourth century by Hindu philosopher Mallanaga Vatsyayana, it's considered the Bible of sex positions, describing all of them in detail, with each one designed as a way to "activate energy." It was initially created to make for a more spiritual experience for the upper-caste male, and not as a sex-position book for the masses, as it came to be. The book—still selling thousands of copies annually—has incited giggles from prepubescent boys, fascinated pretentious art history students and provided a nucleus of information for people whose curiosity gets the best of them. The book has had a massive influence on the eager, naughty and nasty in today's bedrooms. There are even modern-day versions of it, like *Playboy*'s "Sex Position of the Day," *Carma Sutra* (a book specifically focusing on sex positions in a car) and *The Snuggie Sutra* (yes, sex positions inside that weird blanket with arms).

Somehow, information on sex positions never gets old, never tires and always fascinates. According to the Kinsey Institute, it

The Indians Must Know Something We Don't

A Russian couple literally got *stuck* after attempting a position from the *Kama Sutra*: the Desk Chair, or *Indrani*. In a nutshell, the woman pulls her knees up so that her feet dig into her lover's armpits. Well, the wife got a spasm and they locked up and couldn't move. After an hour of trying, they crab-walked together over to the phone and called for help.

would take the average American couple four years to do every position in the *Kama Sutra*.

Built in thirteenth-century India, the Konark Sun Temple, dedicated to the sun god, Arka, is a World Heritage Site and one of the seven wonders of India. It is famous for its erotic art, stone carvings that depict many sexual, sensual positions.

In the sixteenth century, the Arabs in North Africa were really into *The Perfumed Garden for the Soul's Recreation* by Sheikh Nefzaoui. It was erotic literature meant to be read by men only that was later translated into the English and called *A Manual of Arabian Erotology*. The book's goal was to emphasize that the way to gain ultimate fulfillment is through sexual intercourse.

Yasuyori Tamba's *Ishimpo*, written around the tenth century, is the oldest Japanese medical text that includes sexual healing positions. It is based on ancient Chinese medical advice, and is known as the Taoist sex manual.

Ananga Ranga, another Indian sex manual, was written in the fifteenth or sixteenth century by poet Kalyana Malla with the intention of stopping marriage separations. Heavily influenced by the *Kama Sutra*, the manual taught men about monogamy where one woman could be enough for any man. It also brought astrology into the bedroom as a guide.

Skipping ahead to the late 1800s, Richard von Krafft-Ebing, who conducted scientific studies about sex and all the bells and whistles that go with it, introduced many sex terms in his book *Psychopathia Sexualis* that have since found a place in our modern-day lexicon. Take "sadism" for example: the sexual pleasure you get from watching someone else in pain. This stems directly from the Marquis de Sade, who wrote books about violent sexual activity. Then there's "masochism": sexual gratification from having the shit kicked out of you or being humiliated. In his book *Venus in Furs*, Leopold von Sacher-Masoch wrote about a man wanting to be whipped and enslaved by a woman. Krafft-Ebing was inspired by Sacher-Masoch when he came up with the term "masochism." On top of that, Kraftt-Ebing was the first person to say that homosexuals are "normal" people who are only into something slightly different than what was considered typical.

In the nineteenth and twentieth centuries, Sigmund Freud was famous for his various philosophies, and his books, including *Sexuality and the Psychology of Love* and *Beyond the Pleasure Principle*. Each has had a huge impact on our understanding of society and sexuality today.

The Institute for Sexology, the first of its kind, was created in Berlin in 1919 by Magnus Hirschfeld. The institute surveyed countless people for studies, offered marriage and sex counseling and had a sexuality research library. It promoted equal rights for everyone, no matter their sexual orientation. However, the Nazis destroyed it in 1933. Yet in 1983, the Magnus Hirschfeld Archive for Sexology opened to the public, a rebirth of sorts.

In 1947, Alfred Kinsey, author of the bestsellers *Sexual Behavior of the Human Male* and *Sexual Behavior of the Human Female*, founded the Institute for Sex Research at Indiana University in Bloomington, now the Kinsey Institute for Research in Sex, Gender, and Reproduction. Kinsey was a professor of entomology and zoology who just wanted to talk about sex—thereby getting more people to talk about sex. He was the ultimate believer in the idea

Holy Moly!

The Catholic Church discusses the subject of sex quite a lot. But when Polish priest Father Ksawery Knotz started talking about sex, it wasn't necessarily in line with what the Vatican was preaching. Father Knotz decided it was important to write a sex book, which, among other things, described different sexual positions. Titled *Sex as You Don't Know It: For Married Couples Who Love God* and published in 2009, the book claims the Catholic Church doesn't expect married couples to sit around and procreate only in the missionary position. It was dubbed the "Catholic *Kama Sutra*" and sold like hot pierogies. It also has been translated into languages such as Ukrainian. Knotz is frequently questioned about how someone like himself—celibate—could possibly know anything on the subject. He claims that he has learned vicariously through the couples he's counseled and a website he hosts where he gives sexual advice. But he remains traditional in one respect: he still discourages the use of birth control.

that it's better to know than not to know. And he looked at sex as a history of science. Many were perturbed by his work and research. Today, the Kinsey Institute has a firm place at Indiana University in Bloomington, Indiana, and the Kinsey Report is still looked upon by experts and scientists as an extremely important and valuable collection of ideas.

The research and husband-wife team of William Masters and Virginia Johnson published *Human Sexual Response* in 1966 and *Human Sexual Inadequacy* in 1970. The books revealed a great deal about human sexual response and dysfunctions, including studies on how women reach orgasms. The books were meant to be available for the medical field but they became bestsellers, with the publications being translated into more than thirty languages. There was a Masters and Johnson Institute in St. Louis, Missouri, from 1978 to 1994 (it closed with their retirement). They both were inducted into the St. Louis Walk of Fame.

The Personalities

There are countless celebrities, politicians and other famous names throughout history who have had imperfect—or rather, let's say, intriguing—sides. Sometimes, when private facts about a person are revealed, it is a shock to the general public; other times, it only humanizes these larger-than-life figures and makes the public appreciate them all the more.

For those who still find homosexuality kinky, Emperor Nero (AD 37–68) was the first Roman ruler to marry a male. And yet, Emperor Claudius (10 BC–AD 54) was the only one of the emperors not to take on a male lover.

Roman emperor Tiberius (42 BC–AD 37) was one crazy bisexual sovereign. With ancient Roman porn adorning many of his walls, Tiberius would throw sex parties and get "tickled" by young boys who fondled his genitals underwater. He called these boys "tiddlers" (the Latin word for "fishes") since they were trained to lick and touch just the right spots between his legs. If that isn't perverse enough for you, it's said he would take newborns and put them to his organ, letting the instinctive sucking motion take over. Stay classy, Tiberius.

Roman emperor Elagabalus (AD 218–222) was quite womanly. Not only was he into cross-dressing and wearing a ton of makeup; he even liked to role-play, acting as the "cheating wife" and getting beaten up for it. He so liked "being" a woman, it's said he even wanted doctors to cut a vagina into him. Back in the day, designer vaginas weren't exactly popular so that never happened.

Wife of Emperor Justinian, Empress Theodora, of the Byzantine Empire of Rome (AD 500–548), couldn't get enough. Her Majesty had dozens of slaves brought to her so that she could be filled in every orifice at any given moment. She also liked to have geese scoop up grain from her midsection, and to dance around naked.

Mongolian warlord Genghis Khan (1162–1227), a name meaning "universal ruler"—but probably should mean "universal sperm donor"—impregnated thousands of women. There's a specific Y chromosome present in many Asian men, tracing back to the thirteenth century, exactly at the time when Khan was dropping his seed all over the place. In 2003, a study by geneticists called "The Genetic Legacy of the Mongols," printed in the *American Journal of Human Genetics*, found that Genghis has approximately 16 million Asian descendants. Not only is it fairly safe to say that he probably fathered more people than anyone else in history, but it's highly likely that the missionary position was not the only way he was getting it on with all these women.

Egyptian pharaoh Ramses II (1279–1212 BC) supposedly fathered more than 160 children. Not only did he outlive some of his own kids; he married a couple of his own daughters as well. The Ramses condom is appropriately named after him, although he himself clearly never used one.

England's King Charles II (1630–1685) was known to have indulged in every imaginable sexual act. But recent findings discovered that he had surprisingly taken a lesson or two from his father, Charles I, who was a known cocksmith, "swinging" (seventeenth-century English word for dirty sex) a few ladies on the side as well while preaching against immorality and drunkenness.

In 1642, Thomas Graunger, a teenage farm boy, was victim of the first recorded Massachusetts execution due to a sex crime. Graunger was prosecuted for having sex with the things he deemed closest to him: animals. More precisely, a mare, a cow, two goats, five sheep, two calves and a turkey. In order for him to recognize the full extent of his crime, the court made him first watch his "lovers" be killed before he was hanged.

Jean-Jacques Rousseau, a famous philosopher in the 1770s, had a spanking fetish that was ignited at the age of eight when his adopted mom took her hand to his buttocks. He wrote about this in his autobiography, *Confessions*, where he also stated, "To be at the knees of an imperious mistress, to obey her orders, to have to beg her pardon, have been for me the sweetest delights."

King Edward VII of England (1841–1910) had an armchair of love (called *fauteuil d'amour*) that he used with his prostitutes at Le Chabanais brothel. The chair looks more like a strange, antique version of a bunk bed, although the top resembles an incredibly ornate gynecological examination chair. He could balance two women at a time on the chair and not have to strain too much.

Writer James Joyce wrote letters to his wife, Nora Barnacle, showing a different set of literary skills: he wrote in erotic detail about their sex lives together that were sometimes quite raunchy. "My sweet little whorish Nora, . . . dirty little girl." And there's also: "to fling you down under me on that soft belly of yours and fuck you up behind, like a hog riding a sow, glorying in the very stink and sweat that rises from your arse, glorying in the open shame of your upturned dress and white girlish drawers and in the confusion of your flushed cheeks and tangled hair." While Joyce's heirs did not allow for these letters to be printed, some of them did make it into the *Selected Letters of James Joyce* (1975).

The bisexual dancer, artist, actress and prostitute Anita Berber made quite an impression during her short twenty-nine-year life in Germany's Weimar era (1918–1933). She was known for being the first person to dance naked onstage. With the controversy of her prostitution swirling around her, she took things further, shocking people with kinky performances, her bare walks through hotel lobbies—nude, except for a monkey around her neck, a sable wrap and a broach filled with cocaine—and her drug use.

Grigori Yefimovich Rasputin secured his place in Russian history after he charmed the pants off of the czar's wife. He was called many things: healer (he helped the czar's hemophilic son with his illness), mystic, womanizer, mad peasant, devil incarnate and the most hated man in Russia. And his influence over the czarina probably helped trigger the Russian Revolution in 1917. Among its victims was the entire royal family: the czar, the czarina and their children were all executed—and so was Rasputin. The "mad monk" was particularly known for his large penis—whispered to be eleven inches flaccid. It was supposedly accented with a wart that not only aroused women to orgasm, but even to faint from its intensity. Rasputin's Siberian-size wiener was *cut off* and preserved after he was killed, and has been on display at the Erotica Museum in St. Petersburg since 2004. There's doubt about its authenticity, but those who believe it's the real deal also believe that simply peering at this monstrosity is a cure for impotence.

When the composer Percy Grainger died in 1961, he donated a collection of whips to the Grainger Museum in Melbourne, Australia, which he established. Grainger liked to have mirrors placed all over his bedroom so he could take photos at every angle after his wife beat him, and he made sure to document it, noting which whip was used.

After being caught, raped and beaten with a cane by the Turks, British author Lawrence of Arabia (or Lieutenant Colonel Thomas Edward Lawrence) liked to be whipped by his friend John Bruce. Bruce was then told by Lawrence to write about it in detail, and he did, to the British *Sunday Times* in 1968.

Xaviera Hollander is one of the most famous madams ever. Her 1972 book, *The Happy Hooker*, made her a household name. The book talked about her life as a call girl, hooker and madam, with sections devoted to kinky sex, S&M and lesbianism. It was a shocking read for most people, but it was most definitely informative!

Mahatma Gandhi was famous for preaching peace and celibacy. Known as someone who liked to test himself to the limit, he figured how to do that with celibacy. One way was to take on the challenge of sleeping with naked women, even having them do a striptease for him but not allowing any of it to result in sex. He claimed that as long as nothing was happening, he could continue doing this freely to assess his strength. The thing was, he slept next to some very young girls. Like Abha, the sixteen-year-old wife of his grandnephew, and Manu, his eighteen-year-old grand-niece. Gandhi told her father he was sleeping with her to make sure she had good sleeping posture. Sometimes he'd sleep with both girls at the same time. As Gandhi explained the meaning of his *brahmacharya* (Sanskrit for "celibacy"): "One who never has any lustful intention, who, by constant attendance upon God, has become proof against conscious or unconscious emissions, who is capable of lying naked with naked women, however beautiful, without being in any manner whatsoever sexually excited . . . who is making daily and steady progress towards God and whose every act is done in pursuance of that end and no other."

While Gandhi was dishing out advice to others on how to stay chaste (take cold showers, men!), there were reports, such as in Jad Adams's book *Gandhi: Naked Ambition*, that he was sleeping with other men's wives and having sexual relations with them (and then forbade their husbands to sleep with them). On top of it, he supposedly denied his own wife sex.

For obvious reasons, there are many who squash these reports in order to preserve Gandhi's name. However, books such as *Gandhi: Naked Ambition* have shed a few more rays of light on this enlightened man, writing extensively about his sexual prowess.

THE POLITICIANS OF RECENT TIMES

Whether it's ego or just plain delusion, many politicians show their "human" (or "out there") sides when they get caught—or found out—for their sexual preferences.

It's been said that Adolf Hitler liked golden showers and was even coprophiliac—meaning he was into women's feces.

Mao Tse-tung, former Communist and murderous leader of China from 1949 to 1976, supposedly had sex with virgins because he thought it'd keep him young and healthy. It was an ancient traditional Chinese belief that he chose to adamantly believe in.

In 1963, the Profumo affair was a huge scandal in the UK that made headlines everywhere. A British minister, John Profumo, was doing a call girl, Christine Keeler, who happened to be a Russian spy's mistress. Profumo lied about his involvement with Keeler, since associating in any way with a Russian spy—even by way of a mutual lover—during the Cold War could cost you your career, family or even life. But soon enough, the truth came out, and he was forced to resign from politics (his wife stood by his side). But along with the affair's revelation came a coined name for sexy women's boots: "kinky boots," in response to the fashionably high boots Keeler wore with short skirts. These were long, usually black boots that covered women's legs, sometimes up to the thigh.

Clinton lied. A man might forget where he parks or where he lives, but he never forgets oral sex, no matter how bad it is.

—BARBARA BUSH

Former president Bill Clinton put a whole new meaning on lighting up a stogie when it was discovered that Monica Lewinsky said it'd be okay for him to "do that," and she admitted they used a cigar sexually once. He also gave a new meaning to "sexual relations" when he claimed he did not have "sexual relations with that woman."

Going to sex clubs can get you in more trouble than you'd like. During her divorce from her husband, Republican Jack Ryan, actress Jeri Ryan told the court that Jack forced her to attend sex clubs with him in Paris, New Orleans and New York, and pressured her to have sex in public. When these allegations came out, Jack was forced to step down from running against Barack Obama in the 2004 Illinois Senate race.

The former president of the National Association of Evangelicals, Reverend Ted Haggard, was busted after a male prostitute, who also happened to be Haggard's crystal meth dealer, came out with tales about sordid blow jobs and meth parties. His scandal was so scandalous he was forced out of the church. He went on to sell insurance and continue living with his wife.

Naked Hiking Day on the Appalachian Trail falls on the first day of summer. But South Carolina's former governor Mark Sanford bared more than his soul when he lied that he was on the trail that very Naked Hiking Day, instead of confessing that he was with his mistress in Argentina. Maybe if he had really been doing that hike, a whole different scandal would've hit the headlines.

Michael Steele, the first black chairman of the Republican National Committee, got in hot water when a staffer took a group of donors to the Los Angeles nightclub Voyeur. A bondage- and

S&M-themed club, the staffer apparently spent close to $2,000 of RNC taxpayer money to pay the tab.

Prostitution

When a guy goes to a hooker, he's not paying her for sex; he's paying her to leave. —UNKNOWN

Prostitution, the "oldest profession," has been around since the Code of Hammurabi—the first set of laws, written in approximately 1700 BC. The ancient Roman city of Pompeii had its "official" brothel called the Lupanar. There were illustrated sex acts on the Lupanar's walls so customers could get ideas of what to do with their paid-for sex girls, kind of like a sex-position menu.

In the sixth century BC, Greece referred to government-supported brothels and prostitutes in its literature. The prostitutes were called *porne*, which eventually evolved into the word "pornography." The pornes would engrave "follow me" on the soles of their shoes, making it clear to any man they were open for business. The call girls or courtesans, the hetaerae, were involved in symposiums, where group sex would take place (although the hetaerae weren't into giving blow jobs). These women captured the eye of many men, including Socrates, and inspired many paintings (doggy-style seemed to be the favorite position) and works of literature.

Ancient Egyptians considered prostitutes to be a higher form of being, associated with the gods. Geisha girls in Japan came from a long line of entertainment girls, originating in the year

800. But the first known female *geisha* (geishas were originally men called *taikomochi*—and they still exist today), was a prostitute named Kikuya (around 1750), who could sing, dance and play musical instruments. Geishas were not regular prostitutes; they provided customers with artistic entertainment that usually did not involve sex, although the term "geisha" has often been misrepresented as a form of prostitution.

In 1161, King Henry II of England didn't ban prostitution, but he did set new rules. Prostitutes had to be single and inspected on a regular basis. Then in 1358, Italy not only decided to make sure prostitution was kept legal, but deemed it "indispensable," with the government funding many brothels. Of course, the Catholic Church crashed the party in the late 1500s and fought against prostitution, saying prostitutes should be put to death. After the French Revolution, in the early 1800s, France created a Bureau of Morals that monitored houses where one sold oneself for a franc. Banning prostitution made sense when situations came up such as the Japanese supposedly forcing thousands of Asian women into prostitution—called "comfort women"—for soldiers during World War II. (Former prime minister Shinzo Abe reluctantly gave a lukewarm apology for these actions in 2007.)

Nevada has had legal (but regulated) prostitution in parts of the state since the middle of the nineteenth century, and many brothels, such as the Mustang Ranch and the Cottontail Ranch, have taken advantage of this law. The Netherlands has not only made prostitution legal; the government offers prostitutes health care and other support, treating it as any other form of business.

There are many areas of the world where women are forced

into prostitution even today. Sex trafficking—or sex slavery—is a huge epidemic that is at a crisis level, with countless women and girls being forced to work in brothels, their IDs stripped and threats made to themselves and their families.

> *Sex is one of the most wholesome, beautiful and natural experiences*
> *money can buy.* —STEVE MARTIN

S&M IN PROSTITUTION

According to medical journalist Michael Castleman, in the 1750s, some European brothels offered S&M to their clients. Dominant prostitutes would give the leaders of their communities a lashing or whatever they wanted in order to be a little submissive. Theresa Berkley was an owner of one such brothel, where they specialized in flagellation. She was also the inventor of the Berkley Horse (or "chevalet") in 1828, what looked like a massive canvas on which the body could be spread out in all sorts of directions, ideal for whipping. England's King George IV was apparently a frequent customer of Berkley's in order to get his butt whopped by her on the apparatus.

Tantra

Tantric sex was made popular in the West by Sting, who was misquoted as saying he knew how to make it last all night long. Whether correct or not, Tantric sex became a hot topic. This form of sexual activity started in India thousands of years ago. Tantrics believe there's a lightning rod of energy in us that's sexually charged. One definition for Tantra is "tools for expansion," and by this, the Tantrics mean that they believe in whole-body orgasms, where every part of the human body connects and comes. Another meaning of Tantra is "woven together," bringing together the differences of the Hindu god Shiva and the Hindu goddess Shakti, in order to create one being. Ancient ceremonies included the *yoni puja*, which worships the vulva, and the *linga puja*, which honors the penis. The goals of Tantric sex are to make men last longer and women have more orgasms, and both to have a better sexual experience in general. Tantrics believe this type of spiritual journey is important to increase energy, vitality, youthfulness and one's quality of life. Many Tantric sex workshops, retreats and classes are still going on today.

Oral

When I get down on my knees, it is not to pray.   —MADONNA

Blowing a man or pleasuring a woman with your mouth is an acquired taste; but for most, it's thrilling every time. And depending on who you ask, it can be a very kinky activity.

The Chinese Taoists found it an act worthy of worship. Ancient Rome, despite all its orgies, banned it. The *Kama Sutra* talks about *auparishtaka*, which is "oral congress."

Ancient Egypt has depicted it in its art. The famous myth of

Osiris and Iris speaks of it bluntly. Osiris was killed and cut to pieces. Iris, his sister, puts him back together but his penis is missing. Well, that's no good. So she makes one out of clay and "blows" life back into it by sucking on it. Weird. Incestuous. Egyptian!

As Christopher Hitchens states in his 2006 *Vanity Fair* article "As American as Apple Pie," the porn film *Deep Throat* (1972) really brought the term "blow job" into the dinner conversation. The term itself, "blow job," came from the Victorian era of "below job," as in "going down." We're not a species who toys with excessive syllables, so we now simply refer to "a woman rounding third" as a blow job.

Still today, there are societies and religions that look down on blow jobs, thinking a person's lips should be used only to pray to a god. Judeo-Christians believe it's a waste of sperm. In Islamic culture, the mouth is considered a "pure" organ. In the Inuit culture, fellatio is taboo and something that takes away strength.

Piercings

There are all sorts of body piercings, in every body part imaginable. For the most part, those piercings are a kinky turn-on or a way to heighten sexuality. But this is not a recent trend. Many piercings have their own histories. The earliest pierced mummified body was found more than 5,000 years ago. And the Bible speaks plenty of body piercings, especially as a sign of beauty and wealth.

Tongue piercing used to be a ritual form by ancient Aztecs,

Mayas of Central America and the Haida, Kwakiutul, and Tlinglit tribes of the American Northwest. They felt that this was a way for the gods to better communicate with them.

Today's reasons for tongue piercings are a little different. Many do it just to be cool; others do it to give oral sex extra stimulation. However, the negative health effects are starting to come to light, such as the fact that piercing is bad for the teeth. Infections can easily develop and many dentists are seeing chipped teeth. Gaps can appear from simply playing with the stud in one's mouth. In extreme cases, people have developed brain abscesses.

Navel piercings have always been hot. Back in the day of the Egyptian pharaoh, only the pharaoh himself was allowed a belly button piercing. If anyone else got one, they were executed.

The navel area has always been an erogenous zone. When the bikini was invented in the 1950s, the navel area of the body became a sexual centerpiece. Later on, when supermodels Christy Turlington and Naomi Campbell (soon followed by Cher, Janet Jackson, Madonna and plenty of others) decided to put a stud in their bud in 1994, the craze for the navel piercings officially started.

Nipple piercings have been around for a while. Roman army officers supposedly would hang a cape on rings put through the nipples that were attached to leather armour breast plates. The nipple piercings were a symbol of manliness.

In the mid-fourteenth century, Queen Isabella of Bavaria wore a dress that opened to the navel. This led to a fashion style of piercing nipples with diamond studs, putting small caps on them or simply passing gold chains through them. In the 1890s, the "bosom ring" was expensive, where chains were threaded through pierced nipples. But it wasn't only for decoration; the nipples maintained a constant state of erection. During the Victorian era in England, doctors would even advise women to pierce their nipples to make breastfeeding easier. The nipples would get swollen and bigger, decreasing the chance of them becoming inverted.

Nipple piercings still happen all over the world today, in the mountains of Algeria by the women of the nomadic Kabyle tribe, and many other clans and tribes throughout Africa. And in the West, plenty of celebrities—both men and women—promote this fashion. It's a fun tease in bed, with the nipples becoming more easily aroused and providing a lot more for the partner to play with.

The *penis piercing* was once named the "Prince Albert piercing" after (rumor has it) Queen Victoria of England's husband. During that era, men would wear extremely tight pants. As a result, they'd inadvertently show off their goods and would even place a "dressing ring" in their pants to keep their unit situated on the right or left. Prince Albert was apparently the first to do that, and Queen Victoria was very much in love with him.

The Romans had their gladiators (who were also slaves) pierced in the penis so they could tie the penis back toward the balls to decrease the chance of injury during fights. It also kept them from having sex without their owner's permission.

The early Filipinos would pierce their penises with a rod, attaching things like the large head of a nail on it. This way, when a woman put the penis inside of her, it would not only become hard, but it'd get locked in, with the top and bottom spurs of the rod forcing her to keep the penis inside of her until it became limp.

The Dayak tribe in Borneo in the 1900s had men implant bones in the penis. The *Kama Sutra* spoke of male genital piercing as well. But modern genital piercing is mostly a Western thing, appearing in the United States and Europe in the 1970s.

When the piercing is done today, it's said to make sex a helluva lot sexier.

Fraenulum piercing is a piercing through the "small ridge of flesh joining the foreskin to the glans of the penis." The Timorese of Indonesia would do this for sexual stimulation.

These foreskin piercings supposedly started during the siege of Troy in the twelfth century BC. *The Odyssey* talks about how Agamemnon left his wife, Clytemnestra, in the care of the singer Demodocus because he had been pierced. He knew there was no chance of any infidelity happening.

In ancient Greece, the athletes would perform nude. To help keep things from swinging around too much, the foreskin was tied down by a ribbon to the base. This led to permanent piercing, with even slaves getting pierced as well in order to make sure they couldn't have sex either.

Female genital piercing is attractive in some cultures, and considered torture in others. The VCH (vertical clitoral hood) is usually the spot that gets pierced, since the clitoris can be aroused more easily during sex with jewels pierced in it. But women don't have as many options as men when it comes to sticking jewels down there. It depends on how much tissue and loose skin is available. (Let's hope not too much!)

There are many couples who get pierced together, so they can both enjoy the sexual stimulation their metals and jewels add. Some women have even said that they finally had their first orgasm after they got pierced.

Four

LET'S REACH AROUND THE WORLD

Kinky sex is here to stay. It's out there; it's in the bedroom; it's in the public arena. There are kinky cookbooks, kinky radio stations, kinky coffee shops, and countless kinky advertisements. The idea that sex sells is one thing. The concept that people are sexually active in ways you could only imagine might be the hottest topic in history. And it doesn't matter if you're from the Far East, the West or smack-dab in Middle America: you can't get around the fact that there is in you an innate, whether it be massive or minuscule, reflex to procreate. And that procreation can be accomplished only via sex. Sometimes we look for extracurricular takes on that very thing called sex.

Let's take a spin around the globe and take the kinky pulse of what's happening in all pockets of the earth.

Kink Stats

Statistics vary, and it's hard to pinpoint people on their sex lives simply because they lie, even if the surveys are anonymous. They lie because it can't be easy admitting you enjoy another man's fingers in your anus during sex. It's not easy to concede that you like it when a man's love smoothie is spilled on your chest. So, whether or not the entire sample divulges honestly about sex outside the box, here are some findings that will test your kinky mettle.

According to a 2009 Asia Pacific Sexual Health and Overall Wellness survey, people in India are happiest about their sex lives. The unhappiest were in Japan. A 2008 Durex Sexual Wellbeing Global study found that Brazilians and South Africans were two of the most satisfied societies with their sex lives; the Japanese were still the ones who were most unsatisfied.

The *Journal of Sexual Medicine* found in 2008 that among Americans and Canadians, three to thirteen minutes of sexual intercourse (not including foreplay) was considered to be good sex.

According to a new survey, women say they feel more comfortable undressing in front of men than they do undressing in front of other women. They say that women are too judgmental, where, of course, men are just grateful.
                                                            —ROBERT DE NIRO

Sex Stats

- 44% of women between 18 and 60 have added a sex toy to the mix.
- 20% of men have gotten it on with a vibrator.
- 78% of women who made use of a sex toy are in a relationship.
- 15–17% of women first used a vibrator when they were under the age of 20.
- 23% of adults make good use of sex toys during a sexual romp.
- The average person has 9 notches on their bedpost upon death.
- 20% of women masturbate once every 7 days.
- 20% of adults are into masks, blindfolds or bondage.

According to Babeland sex-toy store, where research was collected from various global and national studies including the Berman Center and Drugstore. com, Cory Silverberg and Durex.

Moving on to more kinky territory, a 2007 international Durex survey found that 75 percent of Australians have had sex in a car. And according to a University of South Wales study, 2 percent of adult Australians regularly enjoy BDSM. In a 2005 Durex study of 317,000 people from forty-one countries, it was found that British men are twice as likely as American men to have sex in public (for example, while taking the bus to work or frolicking in flower gardens). Also in the survey, it was noted that the Taiwanese use vibrators more than anyone (with the United States and the UK right behind them in a tied second place), with 47 percent of their countrymen (of the 2,400 who responded to the survey) admitting to using a vibrator—although Babeland statistics say otherwise, with the Aussies on top of the vibrator bracket. One *Marie Claire* survey found that 41 percent of French have been in an orgy, or rather, with more than one other person at the same time, and 27 percent are into partner swapping. A 2010 OnePoll.com survey found that Sweden has more bisexual women than anywhere else in the world.

. . . Before You Go-Go

Singer George Michael was mixed up in various lewd acts, and even arrested for them. One was in a London park, where he randomly met and shagged a stranger. He also once flashed an undercover cop in a Beverly Hills bathroom with perilous results, and recently admitted to having cruised around looking for sex.

Online sex-toy retailer Lovehoney.co.uk did a 2009 survey of 2,000 people. Their results:

- 76 percent of people engage in kinky games behind closed doors.
- 58 percent of couples experiment with bondage.
- 16 percent of those tied themselves up on a regular basis.

- 68 percent were into handcuffs and neckties.
- 18 percent were blindfolded during sex.

The Americas

Some give credit to the singer Madonna for bringing kinkiness into the mainstream. Madonna really pushed the envelope when she published her 1992 book *Sex*, where Steven Meisel photographed her as a character named Mistress Dita in countless positions with an assortment of lovers. The coffee-table book came out in conjunction with her album *Erotica*. Her ability to send sexual shock waves through society never ceases, with her French kiss with Britney Spears at the 2003 MTV Video Music Awards, cone-shaped bras and a cougarlicious appetite for younger men.

San Francisco, California, has been named the "kinky capital of the world." This is mostly due to the fact that it hosts the Folsom Street Fair, the world's largest leather fetish event, which kicked off in 1983. Its mission: "to create world-class volunteer driven leather events, providing the adult alternative lifestyle community safe venues for self-expression, emphasizing freedom, fun and frolic, while raising money to benefit San Francisco charities." While it largely caters to a gay community, men and women in the BDSM world or those simply curious about the alternative lifestyle also check out the annual event that attracts hundreds of thousands of visitors. They meander over thirteen city blocks during the one-day event, which is full of nakedness, whips and chains, plenty of entertainment and, to some, a truly satisfactory and unforgettable day.

Ninety percent of legally made porn filmed or produced in the United States is made in San Fernando Valley, California, giving it the nickname "Silicone Valley" (a play on silicone breast implants, which are the norm in porn, and the nickname of the center of the high-tech world).

Nevada is the only US state where prostitution is legal in some parts. It's also home to the first legal male prostitutes (or "gigolo" as some of these men like Marcus—one of the first legal, straight male prostitutes—preferred to be called) in the United States. These men work at the brothel Shady Lady, and for 200 big ones, women can have their way with a dude. However, there are critics, like the very organization that protects Nevada's brothels, the Nevada Brothel Owners Association, who are opposed to it since they're worried the male prostitutes will only encourage gay sex.

According to its website, Libido Events, a production company in Vancouver, Canada, "organizes sex-positive events celebrating alternative sexuality." It was founded by Jennifer Skrukwa, who heads more than 170 workshops a year. A working mom, she's an activist and promoter of "sex-positive education and play," who wants the world to know what a kinky city Vancouver is. She's been known to give lectures on anal pleasure and finding the G-spot (giving live demonstrations). She's also thrown massive parties with flogging stations and sex rooms.

Negril, Jamaica, is home to the Hedonism II and III resorts, which host kinky events such as Body Arts Week, Pirate Fantasy Fest and Caribbean Fetish Fest (finding a latex mermaid on the beach would be the norm). The Fetish Fest schedule of events include kinky karaoke, BDSM workshops and plenty of play under the hot Caribbean sun.

The athletes of the world never seem to stop working out. During the Vancouver 2010 Winter Olympics, 100,000 condoms were passed out to 7,000 players—which averages to about fifteen per athlete. Supposedly, the condoms disappeared rather quickly and a new batch was brought in.

At the 2004 Athens Olympics, Durex donated 130,000 condoms. There were 30,000 tubes of lube available as well. There didn't appear to be any leftovers.

Europe

The Swedes have never been shy about breaking sexual taboos. So when their country started selling sex toys and massage oils in their state-run pharmacies in 2008, it was more intriguing than shocking. Problem was, some men were offended that this discriminated against men, saying that the toys were all geared toward women.

Arriva bus company in Copenhagen had love seats available on their buses, encouraging people to flirt. Marked by red seats, if you sat on one, you were basically announcing to the bus that you're single, available and desperate. Hopefully, someone sits down next to you and wants to get to know you. Otherwise, it's going to be a loooong ride to work.

The town of Upminster in England was supposedly the kinkiest town in the UK in 2009. The average bloke in Upminster was keeping it up by spending almost eleven times more on porn and sex toys than anyone else in the country, totaling 70.93 pounds a year.

One doesn't travel to Amsterdam just for the Van Gogh Museum; the Red Light District is known as kink central and a major tourist attraction for people of every age. From sex shows to seductive ladies standing by red curtains in the window to peek-a-boo movie theaters, anyone's curiosity will undoubtedly be fulfilled in this European city where prostitution is legal.

Paris is known for its sexiness, and it too has a red-light district called Pigalle Place. The one and only Moulin Rouge, the famous cabaret that originated the can-can dance and has inspired countless stories and movies, is located there. Nearby, one can have a quickie at the Musée de l'érotisme and discover the French version of eroticism.

The biggest nudist resort in the world, called the Naturist Quarter or *village naturiste*, can be found in Cap d'Agde, France. The nudist section is basically a small town on two kilometers of beach with plenty of naked bodies running around, playing volleyball and engaging in chicken fights.

Germany has always had an underground "bad boy" attitude toward sex. This was confirmed when Berlin was nicknamed the "World's Most Fetish-Friendly City" (a fierce competitor with Tokyo) by a 2005 World's Sexiest Cities poll. Among the countless fetish clubs that vibrate throughout the city, Gargoyle has a dungeon where visitors can pretend to take a time machine back to the Middle Ages and get medieval on one another.

And the fetishes don't stop in Berlin. The annual German Fetish Ball weekend takes place in Hamburg, where fetish designers, models, entertainers and players join in on the fun. Not your typical Cinderella's ball, unless your version of *Cinderella* includes a dominatrix whose carriage turns into a whipping post at midnight.

Asia

Japan has been famous for its contradiction of being a very closed society while being considered one of the kinkiest places on earth. Tokyo's Harajuku neighborhood is fetish central. It is famous for fashion in general, with plenty of artists, photographers and models living there since the 1950s when housing was built. As a result, many people in the area are into *cosplay*, which involves dressing up in costumes of fictional and real personas. Window shoppers can see the latest fetish fashion trends and customers and clients can find some of the most unusual fetishes in the world.

Kabukicho is Tokyo's own red-light district, with love motels, clubs and every fantasy. Naked karaoke? Check. Massive fish tanks with nude swimmers? Check. Osaka is another city full of fetish fame, with plenty of Hentai (cartoon) porn and "soaplands" or "bubble princesses"—bubble baths for customers who like to be washed by someone else.

Also in Japan, you can buy just about anything you can think of in vending machines. You're thinking soiled schoolgirls' underwear? You got it.

Love Plus + is a Japanese video game that encourages men to date women, even if the woman isn't real. The game sets up real men with virtual women—they have a choice of three: goodie-goodie Manaka, sassy Rinko or big-sister type Nene—and the men have to practice dating these "women" (who are on a screen). If they do a good job, the company will send the man and "girl-friend" on a real trip together, to the resort town of Atami. There, the men hang out with their "girlfriends," acting as if they are on a romantic journey together. It's like they have an imaginary friend with them, except she's a computer visual. This is not only supposed to provide the lonely men with companionship, but it also teaches them to remember things like birthdays or to spend enough quality time with their ladies. But some of these men aren't ready to move on to the real thing. The men get so into it, they'll insist on doing things like paying for two people—them-selves and the fictional "girl"—at the Hotel Ohnoya in Atami, not just for one real person (himself). In return, the hotel staff will treat "them" like a couple as well.

Japan's other claim to fame is having proudly assembled the largest orgy in the world. Five hundred participants—250 men and 250 women—all banged at the same time. It was captured on film in a warehouse, and the 2006 DVD is available for sale, titled *500 Person Sex!!*

The first Sunday of every April, Kawasaki, Japan, holds an annual penis festival called Kanamara Matsuri, or Festival of the Iron Phallus. With people of all ages attending, saying the festival is popular is an understatement. Parades dance around Misaki, a suburb of Kawasaki, where a large iron penis called "Kanamara-sama," or basically "Big Iron Penis Lord" is worshipped. The place is erect with penis balloons and phallic lollipops, all centered on the legend of an iron penis that tricked a toothy demon. People come to pray and promote many things including pregnancy and AIDS awareness. It supposedly started in the Edo period (1603–1867) when prostitutes would beg the gods not to give them STDs. The festival today is about celebrating a sexually active life.

Even with festivals like the aforementioned, Japan has a shrinking population, and a lot of that has to do with the fact that people don't have sex as much as they should—and, therefore, don't reproduce enough. Yet it's a country with boundless imagination, especially when it comes to sexual adventure. The Japanese government is so concerned about their dwindling population, there's talk about incentives, such as increasing allowances for child care so the parents can spend more time together making more babies.

In 2004, South Korea opened an adult-only erotica theme park called Jeju Loveland. Located on Jeju Island, the place is particularly popular with newlyweds and is known as "Honeymoon Island." The park is everything a theme park ought to be . . . but with a twist. Complete with sex-toy exhibitions, live models, a penis fountain, international sex-position dioramas and larger-than-life statues of things such as a hand pleasuring a vagina, this is less an amusement park and more an arousal park. The park mascots—a penis (Bulkkeuni) and vagina (Ssaekkeuni)—march around for photo ops just like Mickey and Minnie Mouse.

South Korea is also home to the Haeshindang Park—the Penis Park—where there are plenty of penis statues to hike around.

There are plenty of penis shrines around the world, but another worth mentioning is tucked away in Bangkok, Thailand. Called Chao Mae Tuptim Shrine, it was built as a result of a woman praying for fertility to a female animist spirit, Chao Tuptim, who was supposedly holed up in a banyan tree. The worshipper indeed got knocked up and thanked the spirit by putting a wooden penis next to the tree. Plenty of others followed suit and the area is literally littered with penises of all different sizes and colors, red being the most popular.

Brunei's playboy Prince Jefri Bolkiah has been found to have a collection of life-size statues, some of which are of himself having sex. The polygamous prince denied the existence of these statutes, but it became hard to dispute when photos started circulating, showing him in various sex positions with various women. This is a man who owns a boat called *Tits* and has speedboats named *Nipple I* and *Nipple II*.

Africa

In the Zulu tribe in South Africa, if a couple wants to marry, the parents get a little more involved than what might be considered standard. The parents of the groom call an official "virgin tester" to do a full examination. If the couple passes inspection, they are allowed to fool around. However, no penetration is allowed until the "I dos."

President Jacob Zuma of South Africa allegedly has a sex addiction, and has been told by a South African MP to get help. He has three wives, and had a child with yet another woman (which means he probably wasn't using a condom). This is the leader of a country who's supposed to be promoting safe sex, since AIDS statistics don't seem to be going anywhere but up. And opposition leaders such as those from the African Christian Democratic Party and Democratic Alliance have spoken out against his actions.

Mapona (which means "naked" in Sesotho) is the first all-black South African porn flick, produced in 2010. Because the actors are using condoms, the film was made partly with the idea of getting the message out about safe sex and as a way to warn people about the rising numbers of HIV infections.

This came at a time when America's porn industry was dealing with its own crisis, with actors testing positive for HIV. Shoots everywhere shut down and quarantined anyone who could have become infected.

Middle East

In Iran, if a couple wants to do it before they are married, they can ask for a government-issued "temporary marriage" contract (or *sigheh*)—so that they can legally sleep and be together without breaking Islamic law. It's kind of like test-driving your marriage life. Iranian society overall just thinks of it as a way of covering up prostitution. But then there are suggestions by religious leaders of getting rid of actual prostitution by putting hookers in government-run "chastity houses" where a man can marry her for a few hours—so that they have legal sex.

In 2010, a British couple was arrested for simply *kissing* in public in Dubai and sentenced to a month in jail before being deported from the country. Who caught them in this public display of affection? A two-year-old. And the kid's mother believed her child and had the couple arrested.

And one expat living in Dubai got in trouble for ordering sex toys online. When the toys went through customs, they were confiscated, and the woman had to sign a paper stating that she'll never attempt to purchase these items again or else she'll face legal action.

Australia and Oceania

Australia has a political party called the Australian Sex Party. With more than 2,000 members, it was formed by Fiona Patten, who was CEO of Australia's Eros Association, a national adult retail and entertainment industry organization, as a "political response to the sexual needs of Australia in the twenty-first century," according to its website (Sexparty.org.au).

In 2009, a sex cult pulled a stunt in Papua New Guinea, forcing people to have sex in public and, at the same time, enticing them by claiming their banana harvest would grow bigger if they did so. Whether or not bananas boomed once people performed this PDA is another story.

In 2007, a new trend hit the New Zealand dating scene: vegan-sexuals. These are people who not only don't eat meat, but they won't have sex with someone who does. They feel like that other person is filled with dead animals and they don't want any of their bodily fluids to get mixed up in that.

Five

DESTINATION SEX

People will go through all sorts of trouble just to have sex in places that can enhance excitement. Getting out of the bedroom and finding places that are a far cry from your ordinary sheets can heighten sexual arousal. Maybe it's the thrill of being caught. Maybe it's the sensation of feeling a draft. Sometimes, all it takes is going to the hotel down the street—some hotels today are even stocked with sex-toy goodies. People will even find it thrilling to live vicariously through other people's sex lives, whether it's attending a sex expo, visiting some kinky theater or checking out a sex museum.

From the plains of America to the highlands of Japan, sex can be an integral part of the tourist experience. It's not only photo ops in front of iconic landmarks anymore. People all over the world are taking flight to other places in order to see sex in a different light. Take out your compass, because we're about to get lost in places that cater to those people looking to enhance their knowledge, exposure and intake of kinkiness.

Sex in Public

Since its invention, the bedroom was anointed *the* place for sexual activity. The rule of thumb for most was to hold out until you could get under the sheets. But this isn't the 1850s any longer. Now we're a freer, more liberal and riskier society, and many people today have been acting on the ultimate impulse, dropping trou on a dime and getting it on no matter where they are: kitchen, restroom, airplane, cockpit, office, copy room, courtroom, bushes, and on and on and on.

There have been stories of people taking advantage of park benches, restaurant bathrooms and store dressing rooms. There are even books out with advice on where to do it, such as *1,001 Best Places to Have Sex in America: A When, Where, and How Guide* by Jennifer Hunt and Dan Baritchi. The book suggests places such as a locker room, your hotel room's balcony, the top row at a concert, in line at a drive-through or high up in a tree.

A 2010 *Cosmopolitan* survey asked more than 1,500 people

where they like to do it outside of the bedroom. Answers included: shower and bath (82 percent), car (80 percent), forest (49 percent), parents' bed (34 percent) and on top of the washing machine (25 percent).

Durex offered its own statistics in their 2005 Global Sex Survey, with 50 percent of its approximately 317,000 surveyors from forty-one countries saying they've done it in a car, bathroom and a park. Fifteen percent admitted to working overtime at the job and doing it in the office. And 2 percent are card-carrying members of the "mile-high" club.

THE ORIGINAL MILE-HIGH CLUB

Lawrence Sperry isn't only known for inventing the autopilot in an airplane; he's supposedly the first man to have joined the mile-high club. In 1916, together with his flying student Mrs. Waldo Polk, he took humping to new heights. Hilariously, the plane crashed but they survived. Rescue teams found the wreckage and two buck naked people explaining that the accident somehow tore off their clothes.

There are charter flights available now that offer mile-high flights, where you can have the privacy you need in order to become a member. But sometimes, joining the mile-high club can be tricky—and it even can have harsh consequences. Qantas stewardess Lisa Robertson learned this the *difficult* way when she was fired for engaging with Ralph Fiennes in a bathroom at 35,000 feet.

BALL GAMES

A couple at a 2010 Chicago White Sox baseball game was caught having sex in the stadium bathroom. When the two exhibitionists came out, most of the people waiting in line cheered them.

Another couple was filmed while *scoring* in a stall while the Dallas Cowboys played their first game at the new Cowboys Stadium in 2009.

A ROYAL SHAG

One couple was caught shagging outside Windsor Castle in England. They didn't mind the spectators, the camera flashes or the video cameras whirling in front of them. However, they probably did mind the police who interrupted and arrested them.

COFFEE RUNS

San Francisco is home to the only fetish coffee shop in the United States: Wicked Grounds. They have nights called Bring Your Human Pet, where customers bring in their slaves on leashes and the pets are served coffee in dog bowls. More important, it's a place that brings kinky people together—sans booze—to hang, chill, caffeinate and wax kinky.

South Dakota's Racehorses gentlemen's club is a juice bar, strip joint *and* a movie theater for independent film. The juice bar isn't by choice: the owner was unable to get a liquor license. But he seems to be selling plenty of juice.

A Room with a Kink, Please

Moving on to where one would stay when traveling to all these places in the world, here are some of the kinkiest hotels to be found.

Japan is famous for its countless "love hotels," where people book rooms for a certain amount of time, and for one reason only: sex (usually adulterous and anonymous sex). The hotels are so popular and intriguing, there is even a book called *Love Hotels* by Misty Keasler, who photographed the various rooms available.

Check-in is like ordering from a fast-food menu board, where you can see what's available, the photo of the room, the prices and so on. Order a #4 and you get a king-size bed with a side of K-Y and handcuffs. Once a customer selects a room, they hand money to a clerk and head to their new, temporary home.

There are various themes in these hotel rooms, such as one with beds shaped like gondolas, spaceships or pineapples. There are rooms that look like a schoolgirl's classroom. S&M themes are a mainstay, with some containing chambers in the room complete with chains, ropes and a prison cell. There's even a Hello Kitty S&M-themed room, with bloodred-colored handcuffs to strap you in while a Hello Kitty character watches from a swing above. There are rooms that have been painted to make lovers appear to be floating through galaxies, and others that make them feel as though they were abducted by aliens. I'll let your imagination probe for a description. There's the "basket chair room" where your partner can sit in a basket hanging above, and you spin her around while lying under her. Other rooms include Spiderman's room, a doctor's office and a subway platform. The beds are all accessorized with the ability to vibrate or rotate. There's a sex-toy vending machine down each hall next to the ice machine.

These love hotels have declined in number in recent years, with half of them closing their doors. But they can still be found, and even in other countries, such as Hong Kong and South Korea. Central America and Mexico have a variation called "autohotels."

There's a hotel in Berlin—Propeller Island City Lodge—that offers thirty different types of rooms dedicated to kinky sex. In one, you can feel like you're being buried alive by sleeping in a coffin. Or there's a room completely covered with mirrors and a room with a floating bed. Or the Two Lions room, equipped with cages to sleep in. Whatever you choose, your night will be quality kink.

In Chamonix, France, close to stunning Mont Blanc, is the Clubhouse. But it's not your traditional stuffy clubhouse. Inside is a room called the Myla Suite, with a giant bed and a minibar filled with sex toys from the luxury British firm Myla.

Sex toys are just another item for the shopping list these days, and are becoming increasingly more common in hotel minibars.

Charlotte Semler, who opened Myla in the UK, explained in a *Guardian* article that: "We cater for people who don't think sex is dirty or freaky—most people just rather enjoy it. Sex is part of everyday life and Myla is part of a new attitude to sex whereby a woman wants to indulge: she might buy a gorgeous pair of Jimmy Choos, a fabulous haircut and one of our sex toys."

Mr. and Mrs. Smith is a UK guidebook of the sexiest hotels for those who are looking to get down and dirty while taking in the country. Some of their picks include the Hempel in London, which offers S&M thrills, particularly in a room called the Lioness's Den. In the room, a bed hangs from the ceiling and is enclosed with bars, with handcuffs available. Make sure you're ready to shovel out a few pounds for the room.

Another recommended hotel is the Grove at Chandler's Cross. It has a Duchess of Clarendon Suite that provides you with a telescope so you can connect with your inner voyeur and check out what's going on in the gardens outside.

The Pool House in Scotland gives good "naughty weekend" packages. If you choose the "Ever So Slightly Naughty Weekend" kit, expect a velvet blindfold and edible body dust. Kick it up a notch with the "Horny Little Devil's Dirty Adventure" kit, which contains such items as hand ties and a camera.

Hotel Pelirocco in Brighton Beach, UK, has a pole-dancing area where you can arrange for lessons during your tourist schedule. Plus, there's a room called Betty's Boudoir, homage to Bettie Page, and accented with handcuffs on a leopard-print bed. Another option is the Play Room, which holds a circular bed and a mirror on the ceiling. Or the Pussy room, or the Nookii Room . . . As the website states: "Think burlesque, kitsch and sexy boudoir all rolled into one."

Romance is in the air in Pocono Palace in Pennsylvania, where you can bathe with your lover in a giant seven-foot-tall champagne glass that acts as a whirlpool in the Roman Towers suite.

Of course Las Vegas has plenty of kinky hotel spots too. At the Palms Casino Resort, you can rent out the Hugh Hefner Sky Villa for $40,000 a night, with an eight-foot rotating bed, Playboy art collection and Playboy-branded pool overlooking all of Sin City.

The Standard Hotel in New York City has been giving tourists and New Yorkers an eyeful. The floor-to-ceiling windows, with the curtains kept open, have revealed various activities in the rooms, such as people shooting porn, getting off on their own, with a partner or simply sauntering around naked. While some have complained about this outrageous behavior, other New Yorkers haven't even noticed it.

New York's Library Hotel may take a while to catch up with the eReaders. Room 800.001, code for erotica in the Dewey classification system, has plenty of erotic literature to read, from the *Kama Sutra* to Casanova's autobiography. Although how much reading's really done in a night is suspect.

The Night Hotel near New York City's Times Square was voted the sexiest hotel in 2010 by the travel site TripAdvisor.com. With its dusky vibe, sleek black-and-white photos of sexy shots and books such as the *Kama Sutra* available in the rooms, the hotel has an edginess that sublimely melts with NYC nightlife.

Hotel Gansevoort in New York City offers a mile-high kit, complete with lubricant, condoms, lipstick mirror and a "whisper-quiet" mini-vibrator, fitting neatly into a carry-on that gets you through security and on to pleasuring yourself during a long flight without any hassle.

The Drake in Toronto, Canada, has room service called the "Pleasure Menu." They partnered with an adult-toy store, and you can order anything from condoms to a $400 solid gold vibrator. Just don't leave it outside your door when you're done with it.

Plenty of other hotels offer sex toys as part of their charm. The Las Vegas Hard Rock Café has furry handcuffs and other Love

What's Left Behind

People leave things in hotel rooms on every visit, it seems . . . a sock, maybe condom wrappers or even a child's toy. But some of these items aren't as mundane at the Novotel hotel chain in Australia, New Zealand and Fiji. There, the staff has found items such as adult toys, riding crops and fake limbs.

Room requests are also intriguing at the Novotel chain. One hotel staffer recounted a client asking that the bathtub be filled with thirty-three rubber ducks. And another made a similar request, but instead of ducks, the bathtub should be filled with red wine.

There have also been inquiries as to what guests steal the most from hotels. In the Residence in Bath, England (self-catering apartments which used to be a boutique hotel), the number one thing people take are sex toys—depending on availability, of course.

Jones products such as whips, naughty bubbles and blindfolds on their room service menu. The James Hotel has intimacy kits, "love packets," condoms, lubes and vibrators for sale in their minibars. The W hotels also have "intimacy kits" in the rooms, containing condoms and lubrication.

The Art of Sex

Museums are on the top of any "to do" list while visiting a city. Why not make the trip more fun by venturing into a museum that focuses on our sexuality throughout the ages? And at the rate these sex museums are popping up, chances are you can visit one in your own hometown.

The Beate Uhse Erotic Museum in Berlin opened in 1996. It claims to be Europe's (and possibly the world's) "largest erotic museum." A patron can view the exhibitions of more than 5,000 treasures, arts and consumer goods from erotic cultures throughout the ages, interactive games and 3-D projections.

Beate Uhse-Rotermund, the owner and founder of the museum, was one of a few female German pilots in World War II. After the war, her mission to create a sex empire began and she opened the world's first sex shop. Eventually, this "one of a kind" woman opened a museum and, hardly surprising, it's been a success. There is even a section of the museum devoted to Ms. Uhse herself and her own life, displaying personal "treasures," such as an official warning from the Florida Department of Natural Resources after being caught sunbathing in the nude.

London opened its own sex-themed museum called Amora (the Academy of Sex and Relationships) in 2007. With activities like the spank-o-meter (which measures how turned on a mannequin's getting from a spanking) and the Amorgasm tunnel (where real people are screaming out their orgasms on video screens), and plenty of videos of people doing it in every position imaginable, it's a trip down sex lane with loads of audience interaction. The Amorgasm tunnel resembles the fish tunnels in aquariums, except here, there are no fish, just displays on sex facts and videos of people's faces while they orgasm (and tips on how to figure out if he or she is faking it). Sex toys are available for play, and help is indeed there on how to find the elusive G-spot (if you touch a mannequin in the right spot she lights up and screams, "That's it!") Better not attend with your girlfriend and lose at that game. For many of the visitors, the day ends in the Aphrodisia Café, which is brimming with erotic cocktails.

Another Amora academy opened up in Berlin in 2009, allowing all those who have ever wanted to touch something in a museum to do it—and to touch something sexy! Barcelona was next on the list to open up one of these sex academies, and no doubt more countries will want a taste of this sensual action.

The Museum of Sex in New York City does exactly what its name implies: "preserve and present the history, evolution and cultural significance of human sexuality." It opened in 2002 and has featured special exhibitions such as the "Sex Lives of Animals," "History of Porn, Sex and the Moving Image," "Sex Lives of Robots" and "Kink: Geography of the Erotic Imagination." The Midtown museum is accented with items such as New York dominatrix Domina M.'s brushed-steel bondage machine, a glow-in-the-dark vagina, and a dress made of 1,200 hand-dyed condoms. There's also an aphrodisiac-themed café, and fun warnings like, "Please do not touch, lick, stroke or mount the exhibits." Hey, you've been warned!

Art is for art's sake. Even when it comes to naked people standing around and posing—as a form of art. New York's Museum of Modern Art hosted Marina Abramovic's "The Artist Is Present" in 2010, where nude subjects stood for hours, putting a whole new meaning on live art. It's not an easy task to stand nude for hours on end, or sit naked on a bicycle, or have a staring contest with the attendees. (What's the etiquette on bathroom breaks?) And sometimes the subjects complained that some of observers wanted to touch the art.

The museum Slavic Birch Bark in Novosibirsk, Russia, had an exhibit titled "Slavonic Erotica: Grass on the Bottom of a River." It went back in time and showed the way Russians used to make love—and not only with themselves, but making good use of their animals and tools as well.

Amsterdam boasts a lot of things related to weed, the Dutch masters and sex. There's both a sex museum called the Temple of Venus and the Erotic Museum. Although the sex museum appears to have more historical artifacts, the Erotic Museum is the oldest sex museum in all of Europe that's still operating (founded in 1985) and is located right in the Red Light District. It gives the attendant displays of what goes on inside the walls of the Red Light District so you don't have to sheepishly check it out yourself.

The Czech Republic's capital city, Prague, houses countless works of art . . . but the Sex Machines Museum is probably quite a unique experience, even for the most open-minded. From the electric anti-masturbatory machine to the Iron Corset to erotic cinema, it's a trippy stroll through human sexual stimulation.

English artist Jamie McCartney decided that he wanted to capture the beauty of women in an unusual way: putting plaster on their privates and making molds of their vajayjays. He then placed the clay vaginas all together, creating the "Great Wall of Vagina" in 2007. What he found interesting was that some women couldn't guess which vagina was theirs.

Other places that have had or still have sex museums: Barcelona, Copenhagen, London, Dresden, Hamburg, Paris, Venice, Kaunas, Shanghai, Mumbai, Seoul and Canberra. And Japan is littered with "Houses of Hidden Treasures."

There are several online museums worth checking out for their sexual content. The Venusberg Erotic Art Museum (Venusberg.de) is, according to its website, the first virtual erotic museum. The Virtual Museum of Erotic Art (Muzeumerotyzmu.pl) is a Polish/English site that has (conveniently) sixty-nine pieces of erotic art.

Kinky Theater

Theater is all about interpretation of the material. Well, no doubt audiences were forced to loosen up when they watched the all-nude Shakespeare production of *Macbeth*. The Washington Shakespeare Company put on the production in 2007, which received mixed reviews, mixed audience reactions, but sold-out shows.

Another all-nude production of *Macbeth* took place in 1999 at a Florida strip club, Orlando's infamous Club Juana. However, police did arrest some of the participants for opposing the anti-nudity law (strippers have to wear G-strings and nipple pasties), and for nudity taking place where alcohol was being served. The police doth protest too much!

There is plenty of other kinky theater, from burlesque shows to midnight sex shows that are intriguing. The international hit *Puppetry of the Penis* (or "The Ancient Art of Penis Origami") involves a lot of penis tricks that can make one chuckle or grimace, like the penis and balls that turn into a hamburger or a wristwatch. *Erotic Broadway* is a variety show that includes phone-sex monologues and burlesque dance numbers.

There are straight plays off-Broadway that involve kinky power themes, such as Paul Weitz's *Trust*. With a dominatrix onstage, underlining the play's subject matter, actors such as Zach Braff took the opportunity to show off their theater-acting chops with a little whipping.

And then there are places that are a mix of theater and privacy, such as the virtual Six Feet Under Club (6FUC). Couples can sign up to have sex in a coffin, all the while knowing that a night-vision cam is focused in on them and an audience is watching. The club was on full display in the 2010 San Francisco's Arse Elektronika's Space Racy conference.

Sex Expos

Sex expos are sprouting up around the globe, like one in downtown Montreal at Place Bonaventure, called Salon de l'Amour et de la Séduction. Running for more than sixteen years, the sex expo focuses on teaching the ins and outs of becoming a better lover. The event has burlesque performances by Canada's top burlesque and aerial performer, Roxi Dlite, sexy candy, sex toys and fashion shows. Education is the main focus, with sex educatrix Lady Viktoria giving seminars with such names as Pervy Play Time and Body Licks at the Community Dungeon Stage.

Asia Adult Expo, held in Macau, is equipped with plenty of sex dolls, toys and porn stars as well. Running since 2007, the 2010 expo had such gems as the Obama sex doll. More than 30,000 attendees partook, an increase of 20 percent from the previous year. China is only recently allowing for sex-toy stores to open—even though their online business has been booming for quite a while. The expo gives customers a chance to see new gadgets, such as the world's tiniest vibrator.

Calgary, Alberta, presented its Taboo Naughty But Nice Show, which offers workshops, booze, education, porn stars and a whole lotta sex. In 2007, 35,000 attendees partook in the event, with more than half being women.

The AVN (Adult Video News) Adult Entertainment Expo is the largest porn gathering in the United States. Pitched annually in January in where else but Las Vegas, it had just over 28,000 attendees in 2010. The event is a show-and-tell for porn stars, new XXX technology and the latest in X-rated fashion.

New Jersey's Floating World (named after the Japanese idea of sex as freedom) is filled with classes, playtime, flea markets, cafés and people of any sexual orientation. For some, this alternative lifestyle gives them the sensation of flying high.

The Venus Erotic Fair in Berlin is the largest sex trade fair in the world, all about showing off the goods in the adult industry, with plenty of naked bodies, sex shows and toys from thirty-six different countries. The big things recently at the fair were organic erotic products, such as natural aphrodisiacs, with the label "Bio" placed on everything. Peter Ackerfeldt, marketing manager for the Swedish firm Viamax, commented on the overall vibe of the fair to the *Canadian* in an article titled "Berlin Sex Trade Fair Titillates the Masses": "It's a new era, new companies, new people coming to the business and a wider acceptance among mainstream people."

Taking Off in the Buff

The chartered Boeing 727 Naked Air was around for a flash in May of 2003, flying stark-naked people to Mexico, where they could vacation and travel light.

In 2008, Germany had a travel agency booking naked flights for day trips to a nudist resort in Erfurt, on the Baltic coast. Passengers had to be dressed till they boarded, and then dressed again when they disembarked. And no worries, hot drinks were banned on the plane. FKK ("Free Body Culture") is popular in Germany, and there are apparently some restaurants and shops where one can hang out naked with no harassment.

Air New Zealand came up with an intriguing way to make passengers want to view the safety video before their flight took off. The crew was nude, except for body-painting their uniforms on, with oxygen masks and life floats obscuring certain body parts. (This is the same airline that is planning to debut a "cuddle class" or "skycouch," where people can book a row of seats that turns into a couch or bed to snuggle on. They encourage people to keep their clothes on, though.)

The Russian airline Aeroflot's staff in Australia didn't appreciate it when some of their crew members put together a sexy calendar—posing naked with the aircraft—for their most loyal

Cooking Up Orgasms

For some, the farthest they need to travel to get new thrills is to their stomach. Marrena Lindberg, author of *The Orgasmic Diet*, seems to think that's the case for women. A combination of protein, fats and (low levels of) carbohydrates in every meal, plus supplements like fish oils and exercise, will mean an increase in what's needed for prime sexual function, according to Lindberg. And soy is a big no-no, as are caffeine and energy drinks. Lindberg claims that once she went on this diet, she not only felt more energetic but was more sexual and having many more orgasms.

VIP customers. They claimed that passengers could harass them in the air, causing a lot of turbulence.

Another Russian airline, Avianova, went even further and did a commercial with their crew in bikinis, washing down an aircraft.

America's Spirit Airlines tried to encourage travelers to travel with them to beaches by putting up bikini ads with the phrase "Check out the oil on our beaches" in 2010. People along the Gulf Coast dealing with the BP oil spill didn't quite appreciate this.

Air Comet of Spain had a crew go nude and the picture went into cyberspace as a way to protest the lack of salary increases.

Ryanair of Ireland had a sexy annual calendar where all the proceeds went to charity; the 2010 calendar raised $130,000.

But the airlines are no match for firemen. The most popular "sexy" calendar in the world in 2008 was the Irish Fire Brigade, selling 20,000 copies that year, and continues to be produced annually—and successfully!—today.

Edible Delights

There is no sincerer love than the love of food.

—GEORGE BERNARD SHAW

Sometimes, all it takes is to venture into your own kitchen and find a world of orgasmic wonder.

Some foods have been revered since the beginning of time as having the power to stimulate. People have always eaten unusual things to enhance their libido, like the "Spanish fly" (a dried-out beetle). Rhinos' horns are still used as an aphrodisiac, and the animal faces extinction partly because of people hunting them for their horns. The Roman physician Galen wrote of aphrodisiacs, saying the best ones were warm and moist and resulted in the person having gas. And thirteenth-century philosopher St. Thomas Aquinas wrote of these lust-provoking foods, saying that the best ones were those that gave "vital spirit." The word "aphrodisiac" comes from Aphrodite, the Greek goddess of love and beauty.

The FDA claims that there are no known aphrodisiacs. Whether you agree or not, there's probably at least one food on the list below that you love eating. Do you feel yourself getting turned on? Whether it's intimacy, impotence or fertility, cultures from all

Raw Tastes

Raw fish isn't to everyone's liking, unless you're eating it off of a human. In Japan and America, models are hired to lie still for hours for *nyotaimori*, meaning "female body presentation." They are decorated in slabs of tuna and eel, ginger and wasabi, and flowers (usually covering the private areas), as hungry patrons chop with their sticks to grab a piece of the raw meat. These models—both male and female, as long as they are hairless—are human sushi platters, making about $100 an hour for posing as nothing more than a (erotic) plate. Customers are instructed not to talk to or touch the models.

over the world have invested their ideas about which foods help in the bedroom. Dig in!

Oysters are the cliché aphrodisiac. They resemble the female vulva and are loaded with zinc (which produces testosterone). Casanova would reportedly bathe with the woman he wanted to have sex with and eat fifty oysters as foreplay.

Chocolate used to be one of the ultimate aphrodisiacs. But since it's become so popular, its mystique has worn off. Still, scientists have confirmed that chocolate does contain phenylalanine and serotonin, which jolt endorphins and make people "lovey dovey." The Aztec emperor Montezuma seemed to know what was good for his virility: he reportedly drank fifty glasses of honey-sweetened chocolate every day.

Fruits have always had their place in erotic literature, and their smells, shapes and tastes have tantalized many a lover. Think back to Adam and Eve, who bit into the apple, the fruit of temptation. The Chinese associate peaches with female genitals. Bananas have the bromelain enzyme, which can get a man's member in working order again. Pomegranate, the "love apple," is filled with seeds, which, according to Chinese lore, can lead to plenty of babies. It also helps that pomegranate is loaded with nitric oxide, which gets the blood moving through the veins. Figs have plenty of amino acids, which increase the libido. They were supposedly Queen Cleopatra's favorite sexual booster. The avocado was believed to be a stimulant by the Spanish, who enjoy its creamy sensuality. Because they grow in pairs, avocadoes were called "testicle trees" by the Aztecs. Aside from that, their levels of B6 and folic acid help with increasing libidos as well.

Vegetables offer plenty of variety, but it's usually their shapes that make them stimulating. Carrots used to be thought of as a great seduction device since they are grown in the ground, which symbolized secret fantasies. Early Middle Eastern royalty supposedly used carrots to help with seduction because they thought the phallic shape, vitamins and beta-carotene stimulated men. Celery has androsterone, a hormone that's released when men sweat—and a turn-on for some. Tomatoes were shunned by Puritans because they feared the tomatoes' aphrodisiacal potency, calling them "love apples." The Egyptian fertility god, Min, was thought to have gotten a hard-on with lettuce. Asparagus has a somewhat erotic shape (although on the skinny side!). According to Bert Greene, in nineteenth-century France, a bridegroom's prenuptial dinner had to include three courses of warm asparagus. Onions have had a strong place in history as voluptuous vegetables. Egyptian priests weren't even allowed to eat them lest they be suddenly tempted by desire.

Garlic has always been considered an aphrodisiac in many cultures. It's been known to stimulate blood flow and get libidos charged up, plus ease colds and heal heart ailments. *Saffron* supposedly heightens sensitivity in erogenous zones. *Cayenne pepper* was and is still used on penises to supposedly increase their size. *Aniseed* was sucked on by the Greeks and Romans, who thought it to have the ability to increase desire. The *ginkgo nut* is known to kick-start blood circulation, which in turn affects the brain and erogenous zones. Chinese herbal medicine uses this nut to set erotic desires in motion. *Ginseng* (like chocolate) releases serotonin, which makes a person happier, and therefore more relaxed about feeling the love. And *almonds* have always had a place as a love enhancer.

The writer Alexandre Dumas believed in them so much, he would eat a bowl of almond soup before encountering one of his mistresses.

Honey is supposed to be the nectar that came from Aphrodite. The word "honeymoon" originated when European newlyweds would drink honey wine for the first month of marriage to make sure their sexual stamina was in top working order.

Fish has plenty of bonuses with its abundance of omega-3 fatty acids. And this means that fish (and free-range beef and chicken) are high in L-arginine, which causes more blood to flow to the penis and, hence, better erections.

Pork. Pork? According to Argentina's president, Cristina Fernández de Kirchner, in 2010, pork is another version of Viagra. However, the country had been having a pork crisis, where people were eating less of it, and some think that Fernández's observation was more calculated than romantic.

Fun with Food

There are websites that suggest how one can masturbate with food. One, called simply LetsMasturbate.com, suggests a man can do it with a squid (after cleaning out its insides), spam and heated salami. There is also a fetish for this, called "sitophilia," where people use food for sex. One example is cutting a hole in the middle of a paper plate, adjusting it around the penis, then putting spaghetti all around it, so that you're ready to eat *all* of it!

In general, getting drunk on any type of alcohol isn't the best way to attract sexiness. There's nothing kinky or hot about a man with dried vomit on his shirt. Some kinky clubs limit their alcoholic beverages—if they have any at all—in order to encourage complete awareness of what their customers are doing. Shakespeare famously said about alcohol, "It provokes the desire, but it takes away the performance."

Champagne has always had its charm during romance. Scientists have studied it, finding that it influences certain parts of the brain by uninhibiting them. It's a fun, bubbly drink to watch being poured in flutes or on people (it was said that it was Marilyn Monroe's drink of choice, and she once filled up her tub with 350 bottles of the bubbly). Casanova isn't the only one who realized it was a good thing to encourage his conquests to drink it.

One nonalcoholic stimulator is *coffee*. According to a 2010 survey commissioned by AXE men's grooming products, women in New York are turned on by men who smell like they just had a cup of joe.

The Smells

Odors have always been known to be aphrodisiacs, stimulating nerve endings in not just the nose. Dr. Rachel Herz, Brown University's olfactory expert, conducted studies that concluded the most important aspect for a woman to be attracted to a man is their scent.

The previously mentioned 2010 survey by AXE of just over 1,000 women ages eighteen through thirty-four found that women in Los Angeles were into lavender (how many straight guys smell like lavender?); in Dallas, women are fond of smoke, but not cigarettes or pot; and in Philadelphia, women get wet when they smell clean laundry. A fourth of the women surveyed admitted to not changing their bedsheets a month after a guy lay in them so that they could still smell him. And one other result of the survey: more than half of women nationwide said if a guy smells like her dad (that is, he wears his cologne), he's getting the boot.

In short, if you want to see women's panties on your bedroom floor, some odors that help are lavender, licorice, chocolate, campfires, doughnuts, pumpkin pie and Tide with bleach.

Six

EQUIP AND BRACE YOURSELF

et's talk equipment. Sure, you can find a lot right in your kitchen (Angelina Jolie talked about using knives one night during sex play as a teen). But why not go to the experts and check out the sex shops? Riding crops, genital piercings, head gear, leashes, slings, swings, paddles and blindfolds are just a few of the items you can use to turn sex on its head. What do all these things do and who and why did someone invent them? It's an industry that's worth approximately $2 billion, so let's get some answers.

What really put sex toys on the market was the 1960s "free love" movement. Hippies and their no-holds-barred sex romps created kinky pioneers such as Joani Blank, who opened Good

Vibrations in San Francisco in 1977, showing that sex-toy stores could be clean, elegant and accessible. Now countries like Sweden have sex toys available at their local pharmacies. Plenty of people make a living selling sex toys by going house-to-house and hosting gatherings where they show off their goods. Prime-time television has even begun airing sex-toy ads in the United States. For example, the Trojan brand showed off their newest vibrator, the Tri-Phoria, on TV as a mock pharmaceutical commercial; it warned that the product may cause side effects of "screams of ecstasy" and "curled toes." Most sex-toy users will agree that these wanton wands are a great way to relieve stress, help with orgasms and make a dull sexual relationship vibrant . . . overnight.

But you don't have to spend money on overpriced toys. Countless objects in your kitchen, basement and spice rack can be used for sex. Once you realize that, you'll never look at carrots, pepper grinders or washing machines the same way. Plus, there are more and more sex companies, such as LELO, Fun Factory and Vibratex Inc.,

Cutting Through the Fat

One Maryland woman ended up in the hospital as a result of her partner using a homemade sex toy on her. The toy, a sex device attached to a power tool called a sabre saw, cut into the woman. The woman pointed no fingers after the mishap, and admitted that it was her idea to try out this device.

creating new designs that are ergonomically correct, ecologically conscious and toxin-free. Let's glance at some of the popular—and some lesser-known—items people use to help them get it on.

Dildos

The dildo's had a long history. Soon after the wheel was invented, *Homo sapiens* figured out that substituting their caveman's dong with a phallic-looking bone or stick could quickly start a fire. Plenty of evidence and artifacts prove this to be the case.

Around 30,000 years ago, in the Upper Paleolithic period in Ulm, Germany, in the Hohle Fels Cave, a stone sex aid was found, eight inches long and one and a half wide. The dildo even had a penile ring etched into it on one end. While it could have been a fertility symbol, its measurements make scientists think it would be more likely that it was used as a sex toy. During this time, another possible archaic sex toy was found in the Gorge d'Enfer region in France, only this dildo had a double-ended baton on it. Swedish archaeologists also discovered what they believe to be a prehistoric sex toy, a dildo made out of antler bone, around 5000 BC. Does that mean Neanderthal men weren't getting the job done in the cave?

The Egyptians, Hindus, Pakistanis and Greeks made plenty of use of dildos throughout history. The dildos themselves were made of anything from unripe bananas to resin-coated camel dung. Around 500 BC, stone, leather and wood dildos, or "olisbos," were sold by the Greeks to lonely women, particularly in the seaport town of Miletus. There are plenty of ancient vases depicting artwork where the women are pleasuring themselves with tools, especially while their husbands were at war. There's even a sixth-century BC vase depicting a woman being dildo'd by a man while she blows another guy.

The word "dildo" was coined around AD 1400, originating from the Latin "dilatare," which means "to open wide" and Renaissance Italy's "diletto," meaning "delight." The material used then was wood or leather, and olive oil was used as a lubricant. In 1844, rubber was vulcanized, which meant dildos became more durable. Today, you can buy silicone dildos with a "dual core" so it feels exactly like a penis. You can even strap them on to throw other participants a curveball. Dildos are now made with harnesses that attach to the waist, chin or thigh areas. There are

Let It Flow

In sixteenth- through eighteenth-century Japan, shunga art depicted female ejaculation. *Shunga* itself means "picture of spring." It was popular and classic erotic art. Female ejaculation was considered to be an aphrodisiac, in that if you drank it, you'd become strong, healthy and forever young. The Japanese decided to build a bowl to catch the special elixir . . . and not just any old bowl. It was called a *harikata*, and it had a dildo attached to it to help the woman get in the mood.

"wall bangers"—suction-cup dildos for stand-by action. And the Vamp is a hot-selling dildo today probably because of the *Twilight* and *True Blood* mania sweeping the nation. Made to look deathly white, as if the moon were casting a pale hue upon on it, it also sparkles in the sunlight.

Vibrators

The first vibrator came onto the scene in 1869, invented by American physician George Taylor, MD. The steam-powered and ominous apparatus was supposed to help "female hysteria." You see, during the Victorian era, it was unheard of for a woman to be sexually aroused. Doctors realized that when they rubbed their vulvas, causing them to come, this calmed the women down. But women kept coming back for more "treatments," and thus, the invention of the vibrator helped give these doctors' hands a break from manually working on these women.

There were also hand-cranked vibrators until electricity came along. In 1882, the first electromechanical vibrator was invented, which had a few vibrating options. The first vibrator ad in America ran in 1899, stating that the product, called the Vibratile, would cure headaches, wrinkles and pain. Soon after, the home vibrator became hugely popular, and in 1921, ads were suggesting men buy their ladies these relaxation devices. Then the porn industry caught wind of this remarkable innovation, and they promptly integrated it into their films. This, in turn, shut down the ads for vibrators since it was harder to justify as something to use as a "cure." As of 1952 the vibrator was no longer allowed to be called a medical device—although it is still disguised today as "massagers" when sold in mainstream stores.

Manufacturers didn't figure out how to make vibrators with softer plastics until the 1980s. Then in 1998, the hugely successful HBO series *Sex and the City* had an episode devoted to the "rabbit," and vibrators became a regular item on a woman's Amazon wish list.

Today, there are countless dildos and vibrators, of all shapes, sizes and colors. According to Flynt Management Group's executive vice president, Theresa Flynt, pink and purple are the bestselling colors. You can purchase them in a variety of stores, including high-end boutiques with solid gold dildos. There's the Pocket Rocket, which has been a favorite because of its nonphallic shape and its ability to give a woman a hard-core clitoral orgasm. Or the Hitachi Magic Wand, which was originally made for back massages. It didn't take long for people to figure out other uses for it. The Hita-

Three's Company

There's the Tri-Gasm, a toy mainly for women, invented by Loveology University founder Dr. Ava Cadell, which, you guessed it, can be used for the G-spot, the clitoris and the anus, all at the same time. Whoever said three's a crowd?

chi Magic Wand is particularly popular for solo play since it's a bit bulky for partner play. The Tantus Niagara Twilight Vibrator recommends its customers use it "cold." Even though the *Twilight* series emphasizes abstinence, the name hasn't hurt sales of this vibrator. And there's also the Obamarator, a vibrator named after the forty-fourth president of the United States, Barack Obama. As stated on the website, this could be "your personal stimulus package."

For the truly adventurous, there are remote-controlled vibrating panties, with a tiny vibrator that will turn a woman on while being controlled by her lover down the hall. There are waterproof vibrators that make bath time much more fun. And there are the Pendant Vibes, tiny vibrators that look like innocent jewelry but can still do the trick! (And there are gadgets simulating vibrators such as the Slightest Touch, that uses electrode pads and can arouse a woman to near orgasm without touching her genitals.)

Death by Vibrator

A thirty-year-old British nanny, Nicola Paginton, died while pleasuring herself with a vibrator and watching a porno. According to the coroner, her cause of death was sudden heart arrhythmia combined with her state of arousal. Her heart couldn't keep up with her libido.

Lube Jobs

Lubricants are essential for sexually active people. And the choices have come a long way since the old days when in 2000 BC aloe was used by Egyptians during sex. Then, later, olive oil was used as Roman lube in 350 BC. In 1927, K-Y Jelly was invented for use during pelvic exams and sold only to doctors. But devious miscreants caught wind of it and in the 1980s it was trending as a sex aid.

Today, there are different varieties to choose from: Water-based lube doesn't stain and absorbs quickly. Silicone lube is slippery, doesn't evaporate (a lot of people like it particularly for anal sex because it doesn't dry out) and is second in popularity to water-based. Oils are also used today, but they can be heavy and are

Drive-Thru

Alabama opened a sex store drive-thru in 2010, making it the first of its kind in the world, all happening in the last US state that has a ban on selling sex toys, unless they are for "a bona fide medical, scientific, educational, legislative, judicial or law enforcement purpose." Sherri Williams, owner of Pleasures sex-toy store, managed to fight in court to keep the shop open under these conditions, and customers have to fill out a health questionnaire to justify buying any of the products. *Are you having any side effects using those vibrators?*

often avoided. There are also massage oils, flavored lube, creams and lotions. There are condoms—such as Trojan's Fire and Ice, which has a warm and tingly lubricant on it, offering different sensations. Or of course, the simplest way of greasing the flesh rails is using one's saliva. Many people use this last technique but don't realize that human spit has 500 million bacterial cells per milliliter.

Sex Dolls

Most kids growing up played with dolls. Those dolls became their friend, someone they could dress up, play with, sleep with, do anything to and know that that doll was trustworthy and wouldn't reject them in any way.

As most people grow up and mature, they recognize this infantile behavior and relegate these dolls to the attic. But for some people, things don't really change. "Dolls" remain in many people's lives but with a different set of rules.

There are companies that recognize this need and make blow-up dolls for these customers. They're usually available in sex shops, and are often bought for bachelor and bachelorette parties. But some companies have taken things to the next level. And why not? Mannequins and lifelike figures have always been intriguing to the niche market. And finding one you can live with, without the hassle of rejection or finding out that you're not each other's soul mate or that she snores at night, seems too good to be true.

Movies like *The Stepford Wives, Mannequin* and *Blade Runner* have touched on relationships with androids or synthetic beings that are animated. And in our reality, there are people who seek this type of perfection.

Sex dolls have been around for a while. During World War II, in 1941, Nazi Germany created Borghild, the world's first sex doll, or "gynoid." Heinrich Himmler had it produced to help his storm troopers relieve sexual tension. This "field-hygienic project" was meant as an alternative to going to whorehouses, which were filled with disease that debilitated his troops.

Skipping way ahead to 2010, Roxxxy was unveiled at the Adult Entertainment Expo by the company TrueCompanion. This doll isn't just for some hot robot sex; it's customized physically to what you want and how you want it. "She" has several different personalities, and talks, listens and even expresses emotions. It probably will never need Botox or a boob job. And for the women, there's a "Rocky" male doll too.

Sexy Flotation

Some Australians find it fun to go rafting, but instead of a boat, they hop on inflatable sex dolls. When one couple had to be rescued after their dolls got lost in rough waters, the local police were not only not amused but also issued a statement saying inflatable sex dolls are "not recognized flotation devices."

Other sex dolls include the Telenoid R1 doll. It has the torso of what looks like an androgynous child and is bald and pale white. Or if you have an acrotomophilia fetish, there are amputee dolls. Or there's the HRP-4C, supermodel robots that have even walked the runways in Japan. The German company First Androids created a sex doll that not only breathes and has a pulse, but can also perform oral sex. Japan created the EMA robot girlfriend dolls, which are only fifteen inches tall but supposedly gives a lot more in love to lonely men by kissing, dancing and walking. And in Southeast Asia (and probably other places as well), you can find sex doll brothels, where—you guessed it—people pay by the hour to be with a sex doll (or, as they say in Japan, a "Dutch wife").

REAL DOLLS

The Real Doll factory on the outskirts of San Diego, California, is a company that creates lifelike sex dolls, which they take orders for, sell and send all across the globe. The creator and artist, Matt McMullen, came up with the idea when he started sculpting female figures for art's sake. Soon enough, his figurines inspired him to make flexible models, with limbs that could move and skin that felt real. He thought they would make great storefront mannequins until he posted photos of them online and started getting requests from men around the world, asking if these were sex dolls. Things fell into place and the rest is history. Yes, McMullen personally tested all of the parts when he made the initial molds; no, he does not hire "doll testers"; and, yes, he does get a large number of offers for that. Customers can get a personalized doll, although it's a hefty cost to have a duplicate of your ex-girlfriend made (but it would mean more shag and less nag).

Made with a lot of silicone, weighing between sixty and eighty-six pounds, no taller than five-foot-seven, and costing approximately $5,000 a pop, the dolls do have an eerily human presence. Also available are male and she-male dolls. Customers can choose different faces for the bodies, but the body parts are not interchangeable. Some odd requests from customers have included making a pregnant doll, a very old woman doll, an *Avatar* doll and green and blue dolls.

There have also been requests for animals (particularly dogs) and young children, but that's considered crossing a line for this company. "Our dolls are meant to look like adults of consenting age," says McMullen.

The dolls are sometimes used for more than just sex—they provide companionship. These figurative companions can be helpful for a guy who suffers from erectile dysfunction, a disfiguring condition or any other social disability. The dolls can also be a great icebreaker for couples who want to experience three-ways but not with a real, live person involved. The documentary *Guys and Dolls* gives a glimpse into the lives of some men who have built a relationship with these dolls. And the movie *Lars and the Real Girl*, which used dolls from the Real Doll factory, also provided a look into what this kind of companionship can mean for someone.

McMullen isn't fazed by the kinkiness of his dolls anymore. He does enjoy the work and when it comes to what's best about his job, he claims it's "just having creative license and being able to think of new things and ways to make them better." On top of it, Mc-Mullen talks about the continually growing online community of doll enthusiasts, called "iDollators," where they meet up in the virtual world on DollForum.com. Through that, McMullen keeps up with the doll community and says, "There's some amazing photography out there of the dolls. I've seen pictures of my own doll and I didn't know it was a doll."

When asked if he feels if this is degrading to women, he shakes his head. "They say imitation is the sincerest form of flattery," says McMullen. "All I'm doing is imitating women . . . If anyone's getting objectified here, it's the dolls. We're creating dolls that are objects, not saying that all women are objects. I could talk about the dildos—they're demeaning for penises. That doesn't work . . ."

The Real Doll has dabbled in electronics, with sensors having been installed in body parts and attached to a computer to make the doll speak or vibrate, but it didn't take off. Customers have told McMullen that they were attracted to the fact that the doll wouldn't talk.

If you're thinking about dolling up your home but are not sure if it's right for you, "entry" parts are available. For $1,300, one can purchase just the flat back and torso, which includes a full vagina. Then one can graduate to the full doll. They may not accept your Facebook friend request, but they're open to lots of other intimate encounters.

Sexier Than the Other Side of the Pillow . . .

The Japanese body pillow with a printed Japanese animated (young girls) 2-D character on it, called *dakimakura*, has become more than a friend to more than a few. Some men, especially those in their thirties and forties, unable to find love in human form, have literally fallen in love with these pillows, treating them like girlfriends (who don't talk back, argue or reject them). These men are called *otakus*, which means someone who's obsessive and nerdy. They even like to buy a whole collection of these pillows (unless only one captures their heart), so that they have more than one girlfriend at a time, making them real Casanovas of the cushion. Some have even married the pillow. A twenty-eight-year-old Korean man named Lee Jin-gyu did. He made sure "she" had a wedding gown attached to her pillowcase during the ceremony. Hopefully the newlyweds managed to get some sleep.

Penis Extenders

Seems like men have always had issues with their size. The *Kama Sutra* was already talking about penis extenders. It suggested using wood, leather or gold over an erect penis to make it look better. In 1907, the Penis Stiffener received a US patent as the first American PPA (prosthetic penis attachment). It was made with the goal of helping men with erectile dysfunction (ED), so they could put their penis into a hollow, mental cylinder that had a

Oh Snap!

A snapped penis. Just the thought of it sends chills down any man's spine. Prince Yahshua of Silverback Entertainment can feel your pain. While Yahshua was having sex in the reverse cowgirl position, his cowgirl sat in the saddle the wrong way and *POP!* the main tendon on his penis snapped. Yee-haw.

small hole for ejaculating. Today, there are plenty of penis extenders that claim to work if you put the time and effort into it. The *British Journal of Urology* found that the AndroPenis managed to extend a penis by one inch. However, that was done by extremely rigorous exercises, six hours a day for six months.

There are also pussy pumps, which are mechanisms that basically give the vagina a kind of hickey, making it softer and more succulent.

Ben Wa Balls

Ben Wa balls were used originally one at a time, with a woman placing it inside of her before sex so the man could obtain more pleasure. But then women realized that two balls could be used for exercises to strengthen their pelvises, by placing two balls into the vagina and exercising the pelvic floor muscles (today's form of

Kegel exercise). If the balls fell out of the woman when she stood up, she had more practice to do. Also called Geisha balls, Ben Wa balls are still put to good use.

Chastity Belts

Around 1100 in Europe, the chastity belt came about. Fearing their wives would stray, soldiers used the medieval device to lock up their wives' loins before heading off to war. Today, the crotch lock is something only used in a Dom/sub relationship, with both female and male chastity versions available.

When asked about her relationship with her submissive boyfriend, the dominatrix Goddess Soma explained, "He's extremely devoted and I totally trust him. I also keep him in chastity part of the time. He wears a chastity ring around his cock. It's like a cage. It's uncomfortable but not painful."

Unusual Christmas Gifts

Be wary about receiving a Christmas present from a disgruntled ex. Terry Allen Lester of Minnesota wrapped a gift for an ex-girlfriend, which thankfully she never got (it was discovered in the apartment he was staying in with two other women). Lester had placed a bomb into a sex toy, hoping that when she plugged it in, she'd have an explosive orgasm.

Cock Rings

Cock rings were readily used during the Jin and Song dynasties in China around AD 1200. Made from goat eyelids with eyelashes, they were tied around an erect penis, and the lashes added extra stimulation. This kept the penis rock hard for a while.

Starting around AD 1600, the cock ring just kept getting better and better, being made of different materials such as ivory and jade. The Chinese added a clitoris stimulator, making it a couple's toy, and it's still one of the hottest-selling items today. These rings often had a dragon figure worked onto them where the dragon's forked tongue would be the instrument to tickle a woman's love button.

Today, another one of the bestselling couple's toys is the vibrating cock ring called the Screaming O. And there are the double-penetration cock rings, with an extra dildo to provide a "shocker" moment with some back-door action.

Stingers

The plant called stinging nettles has been growing for a long while. The Romans used it to thrash men "below the navel," according to *Rodale's Encyclopedia of Herbs*, so that they'd toughen up and become more manly. Today, this prickly plant is used to turn people on by stinging the skin.

Candle Wax

Many people enjoy dripping candle wax on one another for the quick burn, slow cooling off and hardening effect. However, there are now candles made with a blend of shea butter, vitamins A and E, and jojoba, olive and coconut oils. These candles, such as the Don't Stop Massage Candle at Booty Parlor, work in two ways: at first they drip down with a searing sensation, and then a partner can use the wax as a massage oil.

Fleshlights and Fabricated Feet and Bibs

Created in 1994, the Fleshlight was invented as a masturbation device for men. It looks like a flashlight with a prosthetic vagina at the bulb end. With a real feel and a closed-off end, men can stick

Casting the Right Spell

One woman in Brooklyn hired a voodoo priest to perform a sex ceremony on her for good luck. The sensual ceremony had candles placed all around the bedroom. The voodoo priest must have said the wrong spell because the candles caused a fire that killed one person and injured numerous others.

their member in, masturbate and not worry about finding a sock. You can order a porn star's Fleshlight designed to feel exactly like the porn star. You can also order a Fleshlight that tells you the number of strokes it will take to orgasm, the amount of calories you will burn and other figures related to the art of jerking off. If you're into feet, men can get a silicone mold of two feet held together with a curious amount of room in between them.

And when a man is finished, there's the Man Bib. Yep, what it sounds like, only it's going around a different neck.

Butt Plugs

It wasn't until the mid-1800s when the butt plug—a sex toy that is inserted into the anus for pleasure—was finally invented. It's been popular ever since. The Victorian era had wooden butt plugs available in the shape of eggs. It evolved into various shapes and sizes, with it continually being put to good use. Today, there are other varieties of anal products including beaded and ribbed, made from all sorts of material such as latex, glass and wood.

There are also prostate milking sticks, which are inserted, and rubbed on the prostate until semen comes out (an orgasm doesn't have to happen). This is a particularly popular device with BDSM slaves. And prostate masseuses, people who will literally get up "in there" and massage your prostate.

Sex Machines

There are plenty of sex machines out there to ride, from the Star Fuck to the ShockSpot to the Monkey Rocker Hybrid. But one worth mentioning is the Sybian, which is regularly ridden by women on Howard Stern's radio show. Invented by Dave Lambert, it's a masturbatory-type saddle that can have a dildo attached to it. A woman hops on and can be stimulated to orgasm multiple times, while the person controlling the speed and power of the Sybian enjoys the full-on performance. When porn star Raven rode the

No Equipment Necessary

Air sex is what it sounds like: someone having sex with someone who happens to be invisible. Think air guitar meets sex play. But it's not about masturbation. Japan came up with this "technique" (supposedly some guys came up with it since they were horny and single—can we say, dumb luck?) and this "sport" is competitive. People compete and perform in front of others, making exaggerated movements, turning sex into a theatrical event onstage, where the performance is all about showing off skills, intensity and usually some comic relief. And, oh yeah, ability. But just doing it plain ol' missionary won't land you the grand prize. It's caught on in the United States, and the Alamo Drafthouse in Austin, Texas, not only has competitions on a regular basis but it also has tours that cross the nation to find the best air fucker out there.

Sybian on the Howard Stern Show (Raven is one of many ladies who have taken a ride while Stern and his crew watched and commented) with its inventor Lambert at the controls, she claimed to have had fifteen to twenty orgasms within five minutes. According to the product's website, the rotations can go up to 150 revolutions per minute and the vibration is adjustable from 0 to 6,500 revolutions per minute. That's a hell of lot of power probably no man wants to live up to.

Fetish Wear

Fetish wear may seem uncomfortable to don on a daily basis, but some people do. Look around the office tomorrow and wonder whether various coworkers are wearing men's rubber briefs, women's latex panties, catsuits, full-frontal harnesses, rubber corsets and bondage bras. Chances are, there is someone at your company who has a kinky secret under their suit. From the late 1950s, when designers such as John Sutcliffe began rubber and leather wear labels such as Atomage, to today where these types of materials in clothing are available in any mainstream store, fetish wear is no longer shocking. Rope bondage artist and dominatrix Miss Nikki Nefarious says, "I love that fact that when I go home to South Carolina, I'm seeing these women walking around with bondage pants, and they're sold at Macy's because some fashion designer thinks kinky is hot."

From straitjackets and armbinders to fist mitts, bondage tape, and blindfolds, there are countless restraints available to keep someone in a submissive situation (to their liking). Here are a few:

Masks: People in the BDSM scene love to get creative with masks. Gas masks are used for "air play" or "breath play," where a person's air supply is cut off and then replenished, as a form of teasing (and can be dangerous). Slaves often have masks that only allow the bearer to see, breathe and obey your commands. *Bondage hoods* are used to cut off as many senses as possible, and keep the submissive guessing as to what's going to happen next.

Collars: Most slaves, or submissives, wear collars to show they already have an "owner." It's usually in the form of a necklace, which can be mistaken for regular jewelry. Larger and thicker collars are often used during play to drag around a submissive.

Collars are also worn in the form of a ring, an anklet or a dancer's waist chain as a way of showing his or her allegiance to the Dominant owner. Goddess Soma, a dominatrix and fetish model,

Silky Scarves

Actress Eva Longoria admits she likes a little tie-me-up action in the bedroom. She told *Cosmopolitan* magazine that "I'm not averse to being tied up with silk scarves . . . I like a man to take charge. There's something very sexy about being submissive."

likens a collar to wedding ring, in that it symbolizes ownership. In the BDSM world, the collar is a commitment and devotion that the slave voluntarily makes to its owner, obeying him or her in whatever terms they negotiated. But this also means that the owner has pledged to be a place of security for the slave, someone the slave can turn to for support at any time, in whatever fashion they—again—agreed upon from the start (it might be that the master must be sadistic at all times because that's the way the slave likes it). The way wedding vows are taken, the same goes for the agreed-upon terms before the "collaring." Only, it's a lot easier to take off a collar than to go through a full-fledged divorce. And going along with the marriage analogy, collaring is different because you can collar limitless numbers of people.

Ball gags: Used a lot in BDSM play, ball gags are held in the mouth for hours at a time. However, there's also a gag that's made of jawbreaker candy, at least making it more palatable.

People are into using these for a variety of reasons. Some get

Just Don't Lose the Key

One German couple lost the key to the padlock that they had locked themselves in in order to be attached to the bed. So they had to call the fire department to unchain them, all while wearing leather outfits.

turned on just by the sight of seeing someone gagged (How many TV shows have shown a hot chick being gagged and unable to call for help?). Others in the BDSM scene find that it's a great way to be submissive to a Dominant figure. And the Dominants like doing it to submissives since it's a way of humiliating them.

Nipple clamps: With pressure and vibration controls, nipple clamps are all about stopping the blood flow to the erect nipples. They can clip on and have laces tied through them. Sometimes weights are hung from the clip. There are different kinds of clamps available, such as the Japanese butterfly clamp (can cause a lot of pain and is usually used by people who are used to this type of thing) or the tweezer clamps (increases tension when pulled) or mousetraps (inexpensive and painful!). Nipple suction cups can also make the nipple look bigger or even decorate the nipple so that

Training Days

Locals in the town of Guenzburg, Germany, panicked when they saw a latex-clad man violently rolling around in the snow while wearing a gas mask and gasping for air. The townspeople thought it might be a terrorist biochemical attack. Meanwhile, it turned out to be just another day in the life of a sex slave in training, who was being punished by his mistress. No charges were pressed since no laws were broken.

you're not completely nude. Or can't afford any more sex toys? Use your mother's old-fashioned clothespin. It will basically do the same trick.

Oftentimes, people like their breasts to be toyed with or even tortured as a way to show they have given their bodies over to the other person, that that person can have their way with them. And this highly sensitive area of the body is a great way to test that sort of submission.

Clit clip: This is a light clip that clasps around the clitoris hood, usually decorated with jewelry and a fun way to keep things under lock and key down there.

Kinky Furniture

Water beds: It's the motion of the ocean . . . or so Charles P. Hall, who invented the water bed in 1970, thought. His creation inspired (wet) lovemaking techniques everywhere. Even Hugh Hefner got one for the mansion. The thrill didn't last too long: sex wasn't as easy as it could be (it felt more slow and sensual than exciting due to the flow), water beds were leaking and breaking, and people realized that sleeping—or making love—on it wasn't the best thing for the back.

Vacuum beds: Many people with a latex fetish are particularly interested in vacuum beds (but they don't recommend sleeping in them). A person is placed in a type of latex sleeping bag and zipped up, and then all the air is sucked out of the bed. The person within resembles a freezer bag. It becomes extremely difficult to move inside the bed, but the sensation is a turn-on for some; others like to have holes leading to their various orifices placed in the bed. Some have their entire head exposed; others leave only a space near their mouth for a straw.

Queening stools: Have your queen sit down on this chair. You will then slide underneath and find an open area in the middle of the chair, perfectly located for . . . that's up to you. But this works great for those who have a face-sitting fetish. Those people sometimes go beyond the queening stool and onto the "smotherbox," where their face is locked in—literally—under an ass.

Love swings and slings: Here one can get tangled up in a type of swing or sling that will sway you into sexual movements with your partner who is holding the strings. From door swings to body swings to sex slings, with padded arm and leg restraints, near-impossible positions and less fatigue can be achieved with these devices.

Rack: This "stretching" machine has been used for years, especially during the Inquisition in the thirteenth century, where people were stretched and tortured on it. The wooden device has rollers on it, and is used for corporal punishments and canings. It's the picture of pain when one is situated in the rack, which is perfect for all the masochists out there who want it—and the sadists who want to make it happen for someone.

Saint Andrew's cross: This looks like a big cross, onto which a submissive can be tied, to the point of being unable to move. Again, in the BDSM world, a thrill for those submissives and Dominants who want to act out their desires, and something one usually finds in a BDSM dungeon.

Teledildonics

These sex toys are computer-controlled, making cybersex even more interactive. Once your dildo is hooked up to your computer, anyone you choose online can control what the toy does to you. The online operator can have his or her own device that is interacting with yours. The excitement of having someone control what is happening to you can be a sexual turn-on. People can even have sex with their favorite porn star, by connecting the film and your toy, which will make the same movements the star is making in the movie. And it can help many a long-distance relationship work even better and "stay in touch" (as long as they have the right equipment!).

Apps

Today, finding a quick lay has never been so easy. You can cut straight through the small talk and courtship and find out who's attractive, available and in the general vicinity with today's smartphone applications. Grindr (for gay males) and PinPointsX are just a couple of the booty call apps that use GPS positioning to find out who's horny nearby. Connect with them, find them and get your no-strings-attached casual-passerby sex on.

Like a devilish diary, users can pay $3 and get DateMate, an iPhone app that allows the user to index their sex-capades. Index and record your last date's info, from hair color to what position they preferred in bed. You can even upload a photo to remember who's who, and you can rate the date.

Apple started allowing adult-theme apps in 2009, but they were already behind. In 2003, the British company Vibelet created the Purring Kitty software for Nokia phones, where the vibrate mode also worked as a discreet massager.

Recycling

Everyone seems to be going green, even those into kinky sex. Dreamscapes decided to launch a sex-toy recycling program in 2008, where they enticed people to drop off their used and clean toys

Wii Kink

Wii released an adult party game in Europe called "We Dare!" by Ubisoft. Kinky players engage in swapping, spanking and fondling in between periods of gaming. Due to its provocative nature, there's no word on a US release date.

in exchange for gift cards and other goodies. The toys are then recycled, and other companies use the materials to create things like park benches. The owners of the nonprofit program, David Kowalsky and Jean Kozlowski, said they created the company "to reduce the carbon footprint of the adult novelty industry."

Seven

THE FETISHES

There are countless fetishes out there. From nurses to the transgendered to commanding officers to people who can only get their freak on in a basement. There's the guy who photographs beautiful models but only dates amputees. There are those who can't stop themselves from making obscene phone calls at random hours of the night. Know someone who gets turned on by dirt and mud? You might.

Studies have shown that fetishes (or "paraphilia"—sexual arousal to things that are not considered "normal") develop early on, between the ages of two and ten, peaking between the ages of five and eight. Children make a connection with an object or sensation and, without having to comprehend it, they can be subconsciously comforted or aroused by it. Scientists claim once they have developed a sexual arousal mechanism, it can remain a sexual trigger for life. Barry McCarthy, the author of *Men's Sexual Health*, is quoted in the 2009 ABC News article "What Is a Fetish?" as saying: "Fetishes usually develop in childhood or adolescence and are controlled by this combination of high secrecy, high eroticism and high shame. It's a poisonous combination." Fetishes can become a serious problem when they trigger a Pavlovian response, where people find it impossible to get aroused by being with another human being in a traditional way. But on average, a fetish is an attachment to an object or body part that's needed for you to enjoy sex.

During the Victorian era, fetishism was commonly viewed as a disorder, and "the afflicted" were locked up in nuthouses in order to get "fixed." Psychologist Alfred Binet introduced the term "fetish" in the late 1880s, saying there were two types of love: spiritual and plastic. Sigmund Freud spoke of "fetishism," saying young boys would manifest a disorder when they realized their mothers didn't have a penis. The sexologist Richard von Krafft-Ebing later made "fetish" popular by studying the sexual habits of countless men and women in his work *Psychopathia Sexualis*. But it really was the Internet that brought down the wall of inhibition for people with fetishes. As Katharine Gates, author of *Deviant Desires: Incredibly Strange Sex*, says in a 2008 AlterNet.com article, "Working Out the Kinks," "I think they were miserable [before the Internet]. I'd get tears in my eyes during interviews when people told me about the day they typed in 'balloon plus

King of Kink

"Porntrepreneur" Peter Acworth is the owner of the exceedingly popular site Kink.com. Sexologist and author Carol Queen calls Acworth the "Hugh Hefner of the twenty-first century" with what he has been able to do with Kink.com. The way Hefner redefined sex is the way some claim Acworth has redefined kinky.

Kink.com has 100 employees and makes $30 million a year. Not bad for dealing with sexy topics all day, where approximately ten S&M and bondage films are on the site at any given time. Acworth owns all 200,000 square feet of the San Francisco Armory, having purchased it for $14.5 million in 2007, and has put his offices there. He also makes films there—where the safe, sane and consensual motto is upheld by interviewing the actors pre- and post-shoot, showing that the boundaries have been established and the participants fully understand what kind of "play" they are doing. There's also his site TheUpperFloor.com, inspired by the kinky French novel and flick *The Story of O*, where the taglines to the site are "BDSM Lifestylers Train Kinky Sex Slaves" and "Watch a 24X7 BDSM World Being Built." His other sites have included Hogtied.com, SexandSubmission.com and FuckingMachines.com.

In a 2007 *New York Times Magazine* article called "A Disciplined Business," Acworth said he knew he was kinky when he was a little boy and would watch cowboy shows on the tube. If someone was tied up on-screen, Acworth was aroused. He was on his way into a finance career when he read about a fireman making tons of money selling porn online. He realized he was missing out, and Kink.com was soon born.

Acworth is not only the CEO of Kink.com, but he lives the kinky life, even starring in some of his site's films. But he's also serious about his business, and taking kinky into the mainstream. He was even recently part of The Economist Innovation Summit, as one of the speakers on the subject, "Innovation: Fresh Thinking for the Ideas Economy."

fetish' or whatever on the Internet and found they weren't the only one . . ." Like in so many other areas, the Internet has connected people with "strange" desires and let them easily coordinate communication, get-togethers and relationships without the risk of exposing themselves to the wrong person.

Most people have a fetish; some are simply more socially acceptable than others: big boobs, small boobs, dark hair, fair hair, red lipstick, white, black, Asian, Hispanic; the list can go on until you run out of objects, features or body parts. Then there are the fetishes that may seem odd to the average person: glasses, knuckles, fur, chicks with guns, wheels, kissing buttocks, etc. There are events such as the annual International Fetish Day in the UK, plenty of fetish parties happening (the monthly Alter Ego party hosted by Fetish Factory in Florida) and lots of fetish literature out there (plus, check out Clips4Sale.com to find a film clip of any fetish out there). This über-kinky lifestyle and condition has come out of the closet and is experiencing a renaissance.

From autaganistophilia to klismaphilia to somnophilia, we're naming a lot of the great fetishes. It seems as though if it's out there, someone's going to be into it sexually. So let's just touch on a few.

Podophilia

Podophilia (or *foot fetish*) is one of the more popular fetishes of all time. Many people believe it starts as a baby. While the infant is crawling, he sees his mother's feet at eye level. Then, looking up under Mom's skirt, the infant makes a connection. Statistics have shown that 1.14 percent of the global population is "into" feet, which roughly translates into 68 million people. A 2007 University of Bologna study of approximately 5,000 people found that the most popular body parts when it comes to sex are feet and toes, with 47 percent of people surveyed preferring them.

There have been many studies on feet. Sigmund Freud commented that feet were associated symbolically with the penis, as a substitute once the male child realizes that his mother does not have the same body parts he has, and the foot is usually at his eye level at that point in time. And studies have found that throughout various centuries, foot fetishism usually rises when there are outbreaks of sexually transmitted diseases, such as AIDS, gonorrhea and syphilis, as a disease-free way to have sex.

People like all kinds of feet, from the perfectly manicured to the arched, dirty, flat-footed and calloused. There are ads in places like Craigslist geared toward those with a foot fetish showing ordinary women or dominatrices offering up their feet for worship, even a little "shrimping" (sucking on toes).

Recent studies done by evolutionary psychologists Jeremy Atkinson and Michelle Rowe at the University of Albany have shown that women with smaller feet tend to be more attractive to men. The concept of smaller feet isn't surprising. The Chinese famously bound women's feet starting in the tenth century to keep them from growing, even breaking their arches in order to shape the foot into the form of a lotus. This was believed to have been a type of fetishism, although many simply labeled it as torture. It was a practice particularly prevalent in wealthy households, where the daughters of rich parents would have their feet bound and therefore never be sent to do manual labor. Just under 50 percent of Chinese women had their feet bound by the nineteenth century, with the practice finally being abolished in the mid-twentieth century. But women with large feet don't need to worry; there is a fetish called "macrophilia," which is all about being into really huge feet, and giant women in general (as opposed to "microphilia," being into really tiny feet—or just tiny people!).

One way people enjoy foot domination is through the method of bastinado. The feet are whipped and hurt, an especially painful practice because the bottom of the feet are so sensitive. It used to be a form of torture; today, it's utilized in kinky scenarios. Miss Nikki Nefarious claims that this is the most popular request she gets from clients. As one foot fetish model, Emily, mentions on her website, RevelinNewYork.com, it "goes to show you how feet are one of the most amazingly sensitive parts of the body that most people generally cover up and ignore."

And then there are those who like to be literally stepped on, sometimes with shoes, sometimes without (called "trampling"). Or those who get turned on by a foot in action—like peddle pumping (yes, a woman's foot pushing the gas pedal in a car).

THE FEET PARTIES

There are foot fetish parties worldwide, with high attendance rates. Partygoers mill around models high up on a platform with bare feet. Photographs adorn the walls of all types of feet. And the entire night is focused on worshipping the foot. Doug Gaines and

Gary Brett started some of the foot fetish parties out there, one for straight people (the Foot Fetishists and Fantasies Society), one for gay people (the Foot Fraternity). The Foot Worship Palace in New York City was popular until it closed down in 2009. According to the owner, "Jason," in an email he apparently sent to customers, the reason for the closure was because the police came and filed charges such as prostitution against him, which he claimed were untrue.

CELEBRITIES AND THEIR FEET

Many people have brought foot fetishism into the limelight. Elmer Batters was a famous fetish photographer whose main focus was capturing feet through his lens. He would shoot feet, legs, stockings, and, through his work, made the foot fetish popular. His favorite foot model was Caruschka, a chunky yet appealing woman. There's also *Leg Show* magazine, which is a top fetish magazine.

Many celebrities have acknowledged their fascination with feet or have given hints that they might have a foot fetish. Director Quentin Tarantino has feet all over his movies but he hasn't admitted he has a fetish. Many of his female stars beg to differ. As actress Rosario Dawson said in a 2007 MTV News interview, "As much as Quentin tried to say he doesn't have a foot fetish, it's like, 'Dude, every movie you have has had great feet in it.'"

Actress Brooke Burke once said, "I love to see a man's bare foot, but it's got to be taken care of. If they're not well manicured, you've got to wonder what the rest of him is like. I don't want to get in bed with somebody and feel his gnarly feet." Marilyn Manson incorporates lots of feet in his music videos. Jack Black told *Play-*

boy magazine in an interview: "They have to be clean. I'm not into, like, funky odors, but I do have a bit of a foot fetish, yes. I find myself staring at feet. I like a heel. If she's wearing clogs, that does something for me. Flip-flops. Sandals. Bare feet are the best." Dita von Teese likes her feet to be worshipped, and they appeared in Ed Fox's foot fetish book, *Glamour from the Ground Up*. New York Jets coach Rex Ryan was tied to foot fetish videos that were posted on the sports news/gossip website Deadspin.com, featuring a woman resembling his wife. Casanova, Elvis and Ted Bundy are just a few more who were rumored to have loved a foot party.

SHOE FETISH

This fetish is intertwined with the foot fetish, and one of the biggest fetishes out there as well. The University of Bologna study found that when asked what item associated with the body was the most appealing, 68 percent of people were into shoes. The fetish is sometimes referred to as "shoe retifism," after Nicolas-Edme Rétif, a French novelist who was into women's shoes and even wrote a novel called *Fanchett's Foot* (1769). Plenty of movies and TV shows— *There's Something About Mary*, *While You Were Sleeping* and *Sex and the City*—have entertained us with shoe fetishes.

In real life, there were men who went to extremes for a collection of stilettos they could spoon with at night (altocalciphilia is a high-heel fetish). People sell their old, dirty, scummy, smelly shoes online, making thousands of dollars. In 2006, the Thurnscoe Shoe Rapist raped women and kept their stilettos as prizes.

Perhaps this fetish is best understood by what Madonna had to say: "Shoes are better than sex because they last longer."

Crush Fetish

Remember, as a kid, squashing a bug under your shoe and hearing the squish? That's a turn-on for some even as they get older. Squashing beetles, frogs and mice makes them hot. However, people go even further with this macabre fetish and step on larger animals, such as rabbits, ducks and kittens.

In the 1990s, Squish Productions, manned by crush fetishist Jeff Vilencia, made the movies *Squish* about crushing grapes and *Smush* about smushing earthworms. But the company closed, a victim of the US Congress crackdown on making it illegal to create, sell or have crush films since it was a form of animal cruelty (even though Vilencia focused only on insects, is a vegetarian himself and finds it hypocritical because people kill to eat meat). Between 1998 and 2000, the crush Internet scene disappeared underground, but has since seen a recent resurgence.

Formicophilia

Find a beetle crawling on your balls and have no desire to swat it away? Or rather, you're actually enjoying it? For those who can't deal with a friendly house spider climbing the walls in your house, this fetish ain't for you. Some people get seriously turned on when they have insects crawling on their bodies, especially their private parts. It's a fetish that's thought to have originated in third world countries where bugs are more than abundant in the home.

And let's not forget arachnephilia, the fetish for when spiders are involved.

Transvestitism

(or Cross-Dressing)

Remember those shocking photos of champion boxer Oscar De La Hoya taken in women's clothing? Well, those were fake but the shock of people around the world was real. It's not often you'll find a macho man dressing up in women's clothing, at least in public. But it does happen.

This fetish is all about dressing like the opposite sex. Dr. Cadell talks about one of her clients who came into a therapy session with her husband, complaining that she caught him dressing up in women's clothes. "Just because a man's a cross-dresser doesn't mean he's gay. It means he likes the feel of silky woman's panties on his buttocks, testicles and penis. It just means it turns him on." When Dr. Cadell asked the man how this all started, he said that when he was a boy, he would try on his mother's stockings and garter belts—and once, his dad walked in on him. His father's anger was humiliating but, at the same time, a turn-on. Now he wants to explore this—ideally, with his wife. So how do you fix a relationship like this—or is it worth fixing? Dr. Cadell continues, "I explained to her that he's still the same person she fell in love with, that this was not a replacement for her. I said to her, would you rather he did this without you knowing? Would you rather he asked your permission? So we talked about boundaries. It's all about boundaries and deal breakers." ·

Panty Fetish

Panties are not a surprising turn-on. People have always been excited by women's underwear. That's easy to comprehend, espe-

Niche Panty Markets

More and more websites are popping up that fulfill a certain fetish or kink. Adam Grayson, of the pornography production and distribution company Evil Angel, owns a site called Pantypops.com. "It's just girls in panties, that's it," Grayson explains. "It's very niche, and the site does very well. My theory on this stuff is that a broad niche competing online, like anal or interracial or whatever, [is hard]. There are just so many players in the marketplace. Maybe we're only addressing 2,500 guys in the world. But at any one time, 200 of them are paying for memberships, which is enough to sustain shooting and a nice margin on that."

cially when you consider that panties' whole purpose in life is to cover genitals.

In Japan, you can buy soiled schoolgirl underwear in vending machines. *Burusera* shops, which specialize in selling anything that's related to schoolgirls, sell them as well, along with a photo of the girl. People have been caught stealing women's underwear out of laundry rooms. Men have kept underwear as trophies after a night with a woman they conquered. And women will spend a fortune to have the hottest lingerie under their clothes, just to feel sexy.

Leather, Rubber, Vinyl, Spandex, Latex and PVC Fetishisms

Leather is big, particularly in the BDSM communities. There's even an annual International Mr. Leather contest that has been

Paying the Price

Edouard Stern, one of the most important bankers in Europe and the thirty-eighth richest man in France, was shot to death in 2005 wearing a latex bodysuit. His lover had just given him a night of kinky sex, but she got angry when he called her a whore and refused to pay the $1 million he had promised her.

successfully running in Chicago, Illinois, since 1979, where thousands attend from all over the world.

There's also liquid latex that can be painted on the human body for extra eroticism. When it comes to latex, these "rubberists" are so into it that they'll sleep in latex clothing, have sex in latex clothing, dress in latex clothing, cook in latex clothing . . . every day. As Goddess Soma explains, "It's a second skin, really. It looks sexy. I like the feel of it on my skin, I take baths with it, have sex in it; sometimes I'll sleep in it. The process of putting lube on, or having lube put on you, is really erotic. The smell of it, and the way it makes your body smell . . . I also love the aspect of getting dressed for sex, instead of undressed for sex." Sexy!

Uniform Fetish

It's not surprising that people get turned on by someone in uniform, whether it's a fireman, French maid or cheerleader. How many times has a "cop" barged in on a bachelorette party, blown the whistle, handcuffed the bride-to-be and then thrown off his clothes to reveal the stripper he really was? Some people really can't get off without a uniform present. Or these uniforms help in the sort of "play" people might be into, like a "nurse" doing needle play with someone or a "military officer" dishing out commands. The alternate reality makes it all the more arousing, and much of it stems from the idea that an authoritative or a submissive figure is taking or giving up control.

The schoolgirl uniform fetish is particularly big in Japan but quite popular in the Western world as well. Even older women dressed as a schoolgirl can have the same affect, since this fetish is more about the uniform than the "girl." (But some schoolgirls have managed to take advantage of this fetish, dating older men for cash so they can buy whatever designer goods they desire—and to wear something other than their school uniforms!)

Vampire Fetish

People with a vampire fetish are usually into sharp fangs, biting, blood and blood sports, since, of course, vampires have a blood fetish. There are vampire cults that even require their members to drink one another's blood. Stephen Kent, a sociologist at the University of Alberta, spoke to the *Globe and Mail* in Canada regarding the trial of a vampire cult, and why these people are so fascinated with vampires: "Some people can feel tremendous eroticism through drawing blood and pain and death."

Other fetishes under the vampire umbrella include odaxelagnia, when one gets sexually excited from biting or being bitten; and hematolagnia (aka blood fetish), which is about drinking human blood and feeling sexual from it.

Beyond blood and biting, there's simply the attraction to the vampire. The original vampire was Dracula, created by Bram Stoker in 1897, and their popularity has not only endured, it's at the highest point today. From the *Twilight* series to HBO's *True Blood*, there's an abundance of vampire fodder out there. Teenagers are particularly susceptible to the allure of the vampire, and part of that has to do with the appeal of immortality. A theory in the 2010 CNN article "Why Women Find Vampires Hot" states that women are into vampires because they are the bad boys who are loyal; "Once his sights are set on her, he doesn't notice other women, and he's utterly unconcerned with what anyone else thinks of his choice." Master Feenix, a fetish player at Bar Sinister in Los Angeles, thinks that the vampire obsession has to do with the fact that, as he explains in an interview, "there is within the psyche of most females (and quite a few males), a sexual desire to be overwhelmed and dominated." He goes on to say that the "bad boy" persona the vampire gives off is a turn-on as well. "Part of their appeal is that they have this wild badness and you never know when it'll get turned against you."

Vorarephilia

People have eaten other humans for religious practices or in life-or-death situations. However, this fetish is about getting excited by the idea of being eaten—or the idea of eating someone. Usually described as a "fantasy" fetish, there are websites like MukisKit chen.com that show women tied up, covered in food and ready to be "devoured."

Taking it to the next level is cannibalism, where people are literally eaten or eat others. Armin Melwes of Germany became famous for finding a willing participant online in 2001 who wanted to be eaten. After chewing up parts of the participant (and the participant joined him for eating parts of himself!), Melwes ended up killing him and eating a huge chunk of him—and then heading to prison for life.

Sploshing

This fetish is all about food, doing everything possible with food, from sitting in it, rolling around in it, or throwing it. The people into this fetish don't mind cream pies thrown in their faces, and sitting in water or juice. Everything except eating it. *Splosh!* was a British magazine devoted to this fetish, its owner Bill Shipton coining the word "splosh." After opening in 1989 but closing after forty issues, the magazine went online, available at Splosh .co.uk.

WAM (or wet and messy fetishism) is along the same lines, but also involves things like shaving cream being applied.

Fat Fetishism
(or Fat Admiration)

This is pretty much what it sounds like. People who are into fat people, who like feeling the rolls and who enjoy sticking their fingers and genitals into layers of fat.

Feederism is the behavior of watching someone get fat by feeding them. There's usually a *feeder* and a *feedee* in a relationship. A *gainer* is someone who likes putting on the pounds. There's also

Body Parts

There is a bouncing boob fetish, where people enjoy looking at women jumping and their breasts bouncing. That's it. There's even an entire website dedicated to it called JoshGirls.com.

There are also websites and blogs devoted entirely to women who stand with their hands on their hips with a stern look on their face, such as Handsonhips.blogspot.com. It's undoubtedly a childhood fetish for men who reminisce about their moms being angry with them.

And there are other fetishes devoted specifically to body parts, such as nasophilia, which is about finding the nose to be a sexual target. Fantasizing about penetrating the nostrils is not unusual.

the *encourager*, who encourages weight gain, and the *appreciator*, who appreciates what these people are doing to their bodies. And then there's the *maintainer*, someone who's put the weight on and decided to stop adding blubber. A *chubby chaser* is a man or woman into the obese. This can be a particular turn-on for those who are also into pregnant women, called "maiesiophilia."

Body Inflation Fetish

Do you find yourself Googling the latest in plastic ass enhancers or cosmetic balloons that are strong enough to stay under your clothes without popping? Then you've got this fetish, and you like the ability to expand yourself in all types of directions.

Capnolagnia

This smoking fetish is all about watching someone play with a cigarette in their mouth. That means how they hold it and the way their mouth inhales and exhales. The exhalation at the end can result in a release for some people. And smoking has no doubt had its appeal throughout the ages, with plenty of ads and celebrities using sex to sell this cancerous vice.

Asphyxiophilia

Cutting off the air and blood supply to the brain can be extremely erotic. Some people like to be choked (hypophilia). Some like to have their breath supply taken away from them, letting another take total control. Others like to be by themselves and hang with a rope around their neck or put a plastic bag over their head and jerk off . . . called "autoerotic asphyxiation" (and the participants are called "gaspers"). This cutting off of air supply supposedly heightens the arousal and orgasm. It was even used back in the seventeenth century as a remedy for erectile dysfunction (since public hangings revealed that men usually had erections that sometimes lasted into death). As we know from the deaths of actor David Carradine (2009), musician Michael Hutchence (1997) and UK Conservative MP Stephen Milligan (1994), this can also be a fatal fetish. There are statistics that 250 to 1,000 people in the United States die annually of this practice where the male manually strangles himself with a belt or noose just before masturbatory climax.

Acrotomophilia
(or Amputee Fetishism)

Lose a limb? No worries, there are plenty of people with this fetish, who only like amputees and get turned on by stumps.

Hustler magazine published an article in 1997 called "Humping Stumps: The Limbless and the People Who Love Them."

Abasiophilia

This fetish involves an attraction to someone who is confined to a wheelchair or crutches, or an allure to someone who has a disability.

Apotemnophelia is similar except the attraction is to your own self being the injured party.

Teratophilia

It can sometimes be difficult to look at someone who is deformed in an extreme way without pitying them. But there are those who look and instead find sexual beauty. This form of fetish also includes people who are obsessed with the Minotaur, the monstrous half-human, half-animal creature from mythological history.

There are those who will modify their own bodies as well to make them look as monstrous as possible. They'll split their own tongues or genitals in half, remove a limb and replace it in a different area of their body, or even get an eyeball tattoo.

Necrophilia

Too many a mortuary attendant has been caught in this act. This fetish is all about getting down and dirty with the dead.

One twenty-four-year-old lab technician at Holy Name Hospital in New Jersey was arrested in 2007 for doing a ninety-two-year-old woman's corpse in the morgue of the hospital where he worked. One Ohio man was arrested in 2009 and admitted he had sex with several dead bodies (pre-autopsy state) while working in a mortuary as a night attendant.

And just when you thought things couldn't go to another level, they can, with necrozoophilia. This fetish is all about being sexually aroused by animal corpses. Roadkill, anyone?

Injured Idol

Perfectly healthy women wrap their bodies up in bandages, pretending to be injured, and in turn, men swoon. It's a particularly popular fetish that manifested in Tokyo's kinky neighborhood, Harajuku.

Dacryphilia

Ever find yourself crying from pain or a broken heart in front of your lover and suddenly, you two are back in bed, making crazy love? He or she may have a fetish for tears, where it turns a person on to see another crying from real pain or suffering.

Fetishy Flicks

There are plenty of movies dealing with fetishes, from *Secretary* (Maggie Gyllenhaal and James Spader brought the Dom/sub relationship to the mainstream) to *Bad Santa* (where Billy Bob Thornton screws women while in Santa gear) to *A Fish Called Wanda* (where Jamie Lee Curtis's character gets turned on by foreign languages), just to name a few.

Vincilagnia

(or Rope Bondage)

Tying up someone can be a thrill, for both the tied up and the one who ties. Miss Nikki Nefarious, an award-winning bondage artist and dominatrix, explains why she loves this type of bondage. "It's about the art . . . What I really love about the rope bondage is every little nuance has purpose to it. It's kind of like telling an entire poem condensed into haiku form. It's beautiful but at the same time there's a lot of structure so you have to pick your words really well to fit that structure. Same thing goes for Japanese rope bondage. There's a very specific structure you have to follow but at the same time, if you want to make something creative and beautiful, you can make it within that structure. It's kinetic art, because you are using actual humans as your pieces. So there's a lot of energy play to it, naturally. You don't even have to touch genitals at all . . . It is sexual, which was perfect for me because it wasn't about sex but I wanted to explore my sexuality. It was a perfect outlet."

For $250 an hour, Miss Nikki will hogtie you, suspend you or just rope you up. When speaking about her craft, Nefarious says, "I prefer perfect symmetry in my ropes. It takes a lot of skill and thought to make a symmetrical harness on some living, moveable, nonflat object and to get them in certain positions and poses where they can still be kinetic. They can move around but still stay within the structure you gave them. [It's] something amazingly erotic for me."

Erotic Electrostimulation

If you like having your genitals (or other body parts) zapped with an electric current, sign up at your local BDSM club, where it's used a lot (and commonly known as "electrosex"). It involves exotic items such as mystims, folsoms, violet wands, power boxes and rimbas.

Medical Fetishism

Remember playing doctor as a five-year-old? What about as a thirty-three-year-old . . . without a day spent in med school? One can purchase all types of instruments to pretend they're a doctor during sex. Enemas, speculums, dilators, pinwheels, needles, forceps and gloves all make the experience that much more realistic.

Shocked to Death

A Pennsylvanian couple was into shocking each other, but it was a stimulating act that turned deadly. The husband had placed clips on his wife's nipples and apparently zapped her too many times, resulting in her dying of a heart attack. The police found burns on the woman's body, and the husband admitted that they had been into weird sex for the previous two years. The husband was charged with involuntary manslaughter and reckless endangerment.

Apodysophilia

(or Exhibitionism)

In the late 1800s, Lady Godiva became one of the world's first exhibitionists. She decided to protest the taxes her husband was putting on his tenants, and rode the streets naked on a horse as a demonstration. The whole town was ordered to close their windows and not look at her, but there were a few who peeked. One was a man who was rumored to go blind after peeping at Lady Godiva, hence coining the term "peeping Tom." It's assumed his name was Tom. Today, the cliché is the man in a trench coat, flashing you on a subway. Or Janet Jackson flashing millions during the Super Bowl Halftime Show.

A similar fetish is autaganistophilia, where people get turned on from being onstage or on camera, usually doing something sexual.

Voyeurism

In comes voyeurism, where people like to watch. And given the amount of porn sold in the world, it seems a lot of them do. People like to spy on others undressing, having sex or anything else that could be considered "private time," and usually end up masturbating to what they see. And today, people don't only like to watch; they like to photograph and videotape, which of course can be illegal. There are countless books and movies that deal with the subject of voyeurism, from *Sex, Lies, and Videotape* to *Rear Win-*

dow to *American Beauty.* It's probably hard to find someone who *doesn't* want to peek into the secret lives of others; however, when it becomes an obsession, that's when this fetish can get someone into trouble for invading another person's privacy.

Infantilism

(or Adult Babies)

This is all about never wanting to grow up and wanting instead to continue being treated like a baby. It doesn't necessarily have to be sexual, but adults will strap on diapers and pretend to cry for Mama's milk. With an estimated 100,000 adult babies worldwide, these adults usually make sure they have no hair on any of their body parts, and will even hire a "nurse" to take care of them.

One woman in Florida was duped by a Craigslist ad into feeding one man's infantilism fetish. She was told by the man who posted the ad that his brother had limited mental capabilities, and was paid $600 week for changing his diapers and feeding him with a bottle. Turns out, the man and brother were one person who was completely sane and into this kind of behavior.

Pedophilia

This chronic condition is when (usually) a man is attracted to children, will watch kiddie porn and basically be a menace to society.

Hentai

The Japanese are known for their kinkiness, as we've seen already. But they are also known for plenty of other things, such as their artwork. Their anime and manga illustrations have come together to create Hentai, better known as risqué, pornographic and even perverted art. The women are cartoonish, drawn into what's the ideal for many men, and accented with a lot of creatures, bondage, tentacles and sex. Google it and you'll find more than 49 million results. It's a popular format, even in the United States.

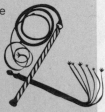

Maieusiophilia

With these people, you never have to worry about feeling out of sorts when you're pregnant. Pregnant women are their thing.

Erotic Lactation

(or Lactophilia or Milk Fetishism)

A person can be turned on by breastfeeding—and being breast-fed. A couple can be in an adult nursing relationship where one (or both, if they are female) feed off each other. And a woman does not need to have been pregnant in order to produce milk; induced lactation is possible with lots of suckling, squeezing and sucking.

There's some pornography that deals with the fetish, in particular in Japanese porn and Hentai (as in "Milk Money," which is part of the *Vanilla Series*).

Acousticophilia

Sounds are sexually arousing, whether it's grunting, music or the simple click of a nail against a desk. Of course, there are certain types of music that are sexually provocative, but some may get more in tune with it than others. And if that's the case, they have this fetish.

Or it may just be melolagnia, where you're so passionate about music that you are sexually turned on by it. Turn it up!

Enough to Make You Scream

In 2008, one British woman was sued for being too loud in bed. Her neighbors complained she kept them up all night and, thereby, forced them to miss work the next day. She was fined more than 300 pounds.

And one UK couple made love so loudly the neighbors complained and they were brought to court. The woman was charged with breaching the ASBO (antisocial behavior order). According to the World Health Organization, the sound of thirty decibels can wake someone. In this case, this woman was apparently screaming as if she were being murdered.

Acrophilia

Afraid of heights? Then this ain't for you. This fetish is about those who find that skydiving gives them an orgasmic rush. Mile-high club members might have a hint of this fetish.

Choreophilia

Seems like most men have this fetish for dancing. From the Hawaiian hulu dance to belly dancing to lap dancing, it's tough not to get turned on when someone is dancing for you.

Aquaphilia

Does someone swimming turn you on? Then you're into this aqua fetish.

This term was first used by Phil Bolton, author of the 1990s online magazine *Aquaphiles Journal*, about the underwater erotica scene.

Frotteurism

Have you ever been on a crowded bus or subway and suddenly felt someone's package rubbing on you? That man probably has this fetish, where he rubs up against nonconsenting women.

Tamakeri

A Japanese fetish where men love to be kicked in their nut sacs by women. But the kickees claim that they are the ones in power since they are telling the women where to hurt them. It's also popular in Japanese porn films, where the customers who most seem to enjoy these films are masochistic men.

Yeastiality

Nothing is as delicious as the smell of fresh-baked bread. However, some people get a little too turned on by it and actually *do it* with the bread.

Maschalagnia

If you're into stinky armpits, then you've got this fetish. And then if you're into putting your penis into an armpit and having sex with it, you're into axillism.

Acucullophilia

A fetish for bald or hairless genitals. Brazilian wax, anyone?

Hybristophilia

(or Bonnie and Clyde Syndrome)

A criminal can be a big turn-on for some. And there are people who have romanticized people in prison, written to them and fallen for them, no matter their crime.

Autassassinophilia

This fetish describes people who need to feel as though they are at risk of being killed in order to get turned on. Feeling your life is in danger and suddenly you have the urge to make a booty call? You're a card-carrying member of the autassassinophilia club.

Armpit Hair Club

According to the *Tokyo Reporter*, Japan had a sex store called Wakige Kurabu (Japan's first armpit hair club), where people would pay to hang under the bushy armpit of a woman for hours, sniffing, pulling and licking it. However, customers' expectations were high and hard to meet, with demands such as the customers plucking the girls' hairs one by one or shaving them with a safety razor (and then it'd take a while to grow back). It closed down after a year in 1987.

Biastophilia

Many people, particularly women, have admitted they have fantasized about being raped. People with this fetish act it out but usually with someone they know, a game plan and safe words.

Emetophilia

Remember that drunk girl's hair you held back while she puked her guts out in the bar bathroom stall? Maybe she was special and worth the experience. Or . . . maybe you just like watching someone vomit.

Bukkake

Derived from Japan in the 1980s, this fetish is about several men coming on a woman at the same time. It was apparently used in Japan as a way to shame a cheating wife. The husband would invite a bunch of guys over to just let them all strap it out on the tramp. There's also another "family" fetish called *gokkun*, where a bunch of men come in the same cup and then someone drinks it. Gargle! It's closely connected to the hygrophilia fetish, where one's turned on by bodily secretions. Or mucophilia, which is about being attracted to mucus.

Coprophagia

Into eating poop? Then this is the label people have got for you (other than "yuck!"). The viral sensation "Two Girls One Cup" featured this fetish.

And if you only like to smear feces on yourself but are not really into ingesting it, then you've got a coprophilia (or scat) fetish.

Flatulophilia

(or Eproctolagniac)

A farting fetish. Usually men are turned on by a woman's gas, and even seek out porn that includes flatulence. And there are plenty of video clips out there to sniff out.

Klismaphilia

While finding animate and inanimate objects lost in the anus is nothing new in some emergency rooms, there are those who are fond of having liquid poured into that orifice, such as an enema. If your boyfriend's constipated and constantly getting enemas, and even encouraging you to do the same, it might be time to be suspicious.

Evil Angel and its founder, John "Buttman" Stagliano, were tried for obscenity charges in 2008 for their films *Milk Nymphos*,

Up Yours

A person's bottom is usually reserved for "exit only" . . . but in a kinky world with kinky people, we can't always be certain that everyone follows the rules. Here is just a brief list of objects that have been found by proctologists and emergency rooms in all corners of the globe: pearl necklace, windshield wiper, Power Ranger toy, cell phones (usually set on vibrate), neon lamp, flashlight, lightbulbs, frozen pig tail, fruits and vegetables, wine bottles, rolled magazines and tennis balls.

Belladonna: Fetish Fanatic 5 and *Storm Squirters 2*. Basically, the films revealed people getting milk enemas and then having bowel movements. The charges were dropped when prosecutors mishandled the case.

Urolagnia

(or Golden Showers)

The act of someone peeing on you warms you up in all the right places. The person peed on may drink it, bathe in it or just hold and smell urine-soaked clothing.

Singer Ricky Martin admitted to *Blender* magazine in a 2005 interview that he likes to give a golden shower—in the shower. He

Some say that a sneeze is one-tenth of an orgasm. But it can be a huge turn-on for people just to watch someone sneeze. One Texas man was arrested for blowing pepper into his colleague's face just so he could get off on the sneeze.

explains, "It's like so sexy, you know, the temperature of your body and the shower water is very different."

Olfactophilia

Smell has always been an important factor in people's chemistry with one another. With this fetish, people have to sniff out people, particularly in their sexual areas, in order to get turned on.

Somnophilia

It's been discovered that people will make love while sleeping. It affects more men than women, and in sleep disorder clinics, 7.6 percent of people "suffer" from it. But how can this be a fetish if the person involved doesn't have control? Supposedly, after the afflicted person wakes, they can't appreciate conscious sex as much as their wet dreams.

Cuckold

Has your hubby ever said he'd be cool with you doing it with another man as long as he could watch? If so, he might be into cuckoldry, which is where a wife is allowed to get it on with another man with her husband's permission because it turns *him* on. For example, one of Tiger Woods's many promiscuous text messages to one of his (many) mistresses, Rachel Uchitel, was about how he had dreamt he was married to her and subsequently found her in the arms of two other men.

A cuckoldress (or hotwife) is on the receiving end of this fetish, and is usually a wife who enjoys engaging in marriage sport-fucking as much as her husband.

Hot Ghost Sex

The late Anna Nicole Smith claimed in 2004 in *FHM* magazine that she used to have sex with a ghost. She's quoted as saying, "A ghost would crawl up my leg and have sex with me at an apartment a long time ago in Texas. I used to think it was my boyfriend, then one day I woke up and found it wasn't." Apparently, she decided not to be scared by it since she realized it was pretty great sex.

Spectrophilia

This spooky fetish is about doing it with a ghost, or getting turned on during Halloween. There's the paranormal version of spectrophilia that includes being interactive and engaging with the ghost. And if you're into having sex with dead ghosts—whatever that means—you're into paranormal necrophilia. According to her website, "paranormal investigator" Gina Lanier has apparently found people who have admitted to having sex with ghosts on a regular basis.

Robot fetishism
(or Technosexuality)

People who love robots, and sometimes even to the extent of turning themselves into a robot.

Hoses and Things

A man and a vacuum sitting in a tree . . . A Polish man was caught with his pants down and a vacuum between his legs. Although he tried the usual "just cleaning my trousers" line, things looked a little *too* strange. The hose had a face drawn on it.

Mechanophilia

This fetish is the sexual attraction to a machine, such as cars, bikes and gadgets. For example, one British man, Edward Smith, knows how to get the engines running. He has made love to more than 1,000 cars, and has fallen madly in love with many of them. Ever since he first sexed up an automobile when he was fifteen years old, Smith has found that his best physical and emotional connections are with cars, not people. He has had girlfriends and even had sex with women, but it somehow never worked out. Recently, Smith put his eroticism with vehicles into fifth gear when he introduced a helicopter into the bedroom.

Objectophilia
(or Object Sexuality or OS)

This fetish is focused on people having an emotional and sexual attachment to inanimate objects.

Parking It

In Hong Kong, a man was walking through a park one day and was suddenly struck with the urge to have sex with a steel bench nearby. After what is sure to have been sensuous foreplay, he soon found himself stuck and had to call the police to help detach him.

Fetishes truly run the gamut, and there seems to be something for everyone out there. Erika La Tour Eiffel may take the cake . . . or cut the cake, that is, with the Eiffel Tower. She has powerful attractions to inanimate objects. She fell in love with the Eiffel Tower and has since "married" the Parisian icon, even taking its last name. Though she had once had an affinity for the Berlin Wall (OS people believe in polygamy), a woman named Eija-Riitta Berliner-Mauer was already "married" to it. Of course these were not legal marriages but more of a ceremony where the women professed their love for the object. Sometimes, that's all you need . . .

Agalmatophilia
(Sometimes Referred to as Pygmalionism)

People who are into plastic dolls, mannequins and other figurine objects have this fetish. The sexologist Richard von Krafft-Ebing conducted a case study focused on a man who fell in love with a Venus de Milo statue and even tried to perform cunnilingus on the effigy.

Inflatophilia

You think a blow-up doll is only for bachelorette and bachelor parties? Think again. People into these dolls engage in this fetish, and are into anything inflatable—toys or balloons.

Balloon Fetish

(or Looner)

Balloons make many children happy. They also make many adults happy. Whether it's touching, smelling, inflating, popping or just playing with them, people get sexually turned on by balloons. There are plenty of websites showing women fooling around with balloons, straddling them, pulling the neck part and stretching it, or just touching them. There are even "poppers," people who pop the balloon and find it to be a form of sexual release (although there are "non poppers" out there who believe the balloon should remain unharmed—and they just love watching and feeling the balloon expand). According to the TLC program *Strange Sex*, there are between 250,000 and 500,000 "looners" in the United States alone.

Furry Fandom

(or Animal Transformation Fetish or Furries with Subcultures Like Plushophilia, a Fetish for Stuffed Animals)

If you see someone dressed as a big blue dinosaur in a theme park, don't be surprised if that costume isn't put to good use back home, where the wearer has sex in it later. People with this fetish have a

The Wonderful World of Furries?

Disneyland is a magical kingdom. Fun rides, mystical creatures and dirtbag nymphomaniacs. A man portraying Donald Duck is being sued by a woman for copping a feel on her breast.

And more accusations are coming to light. Some Disney employees who are paid to dress up in character costumes are apparently not only into wild after-hours parties but also into kinky "furry sex." It's been said they'll don their work attire in order to fulfill a kinky desire to have sex while in costume and character. Gone are the innocent childhood days of looking at a costume character and thinking they're just a sweet cartoon.

close connection to a particular animal, like to dress up as one and/or like to have sex with stuffed animals. There are so many people into this type of fetish that there are even furry conventions happening, where all the mascots can "mingle." The Midwest Furfest started in 2000 and only grows more and more popular. It's the third-largest furfest in the world, with the biggest located in Anthrocon, Pennsylvania. There are plenty of sites devoted to furries, including FurFest.org. Being a furry is a good alternative to bestiality.

Zoophilia

(or Bestiality)

Too many people have been caught having sex with animals to ignore this fetish. (Rumor has it Catherine the Great of Russia [1729–1762] died after being taken by a young stallion . . . It's alleged she died while being humped by a horse. Others claim it was an illness.) People into zoophilia sometimes want to be treated like an animal, wear a collar, drink from a water dish and go full out. Or there's simply an attachment to animals, such as in the relationship Ann had with *King Kong*.

Larry Flynt commented on a famous story from his past. A good sport about it, he said, "At eight years old, I attempted to have sex with a chicken. It didn't work. Kids who are raised on a farm, they mess around with animals on the farm. It is just nature. Someone who has lived in the city all their lives, they might think it's something more than kinky, that it's really sick. But unfortu-

Don't Always Believe the Witch Doctor

One Serbian man had surgery to dislocate a hedgehog from his penis. Why? A witch doctor said he should do it with the animal in order to stop having premature ejaculations. Maybe she forgot to mention some other details.

The Farm

One British man living in Washington State, whose résumé includes being a dot-com millionaire, horse trainer and drug smuggler, had another item to add to his CV: operating a bestiality farm. The man offered tourists an X-rated petting zoo that let customers handle the animals. But Dr. Doolittle's kink kennel ran into the law when one customer died while having sex with one of his horses.

nately, kids who grow up on those farms and don't really have any kind of social life, always get involved in that sort of thing."

Dr. Cadell recounted the case of a man she treated for this fetish. "One client used to come home from school and go up to his room every day to masturbate. One day, he couldn't get into the house. So he began to masturbate on the back porch while his dog was outside. The dog was watching him, and pretty soon, he joined in and started licking him, and, before you knew it, they were having sex. The dog was penetrating him anally. And the guy was loving it. This became a habit. As he grew up, he fell in love with his dog. When his dog passed away, he got another dog and started having intimate relations with that dog."

There are others. Like the Thai resident who got fifteen years in the can for trying to do it with an elephant, who he claimed was a reincarnation of his late wife. Or the African man who fornicated with a cow because he was scared he'd get AIDS from a

One Crime at a Time, Please

While a California man was busted for selling drugs to prison inmates, the cops stumbled upon his video stash while performing a search. Police found a classy home video of the man having sex with a dog while wearing women's underwear.

human. Or the South Carolina man who got caught doing his horse—for the second time! Clawson, Michigan, is a bestialigist's best friend. There, it's legal for a farmer to sleep with his own pigs, chickens and other animals.

Animalistic Attraction

Humans aren't the only ones into kinky fetishes. Many other creatures engage in odd displays and behaviors during sex. The male honeybee's reproductive organ falls off after he lays the queen. It then dies. Brutal.

Lobsters urinate out of bladders in their heads in order to get excited. The male European crab spider is into bondage: he likes to tie his lady up with silk threads. Female bonobos (a relative of the chimpanzee) enjoy a genital rubdown before sex.

Pro tip: If you're a biologist studying the oral sex behaviors of fruit bats, be careful how to debrief your female coworkers about your findings. Biologist Dylan Evans at the University of College Cork in Ireland found that fruit bats enjoy oral sex, and after he told his female colleague what he discovered, he was accused of sexual harassment and ordered to get counseling.

Pony Play

Some people love horses so much, they act like horses, like to be ridden like a horse or ride someone who's acting like a horse. People spend weekends in horse mode. There are all kinds of items to buy for the stable in your bedroom, such as the Pony Head Bridle, molded latex pony boots and crops. And there's *coitus a cheval*, which means "sex on a horse," a practice throughout history when soldiers would take a female victim, place them on their lap and rape them as they rode on their horses.

Loving the Cow

An eighteen-year-old in Indonesia was caught having sex with a cow. He was forced to marry it in order to "cleanse" the village of this "unholy" act. During the ceremony, the youth passed out, and woke to find his new heifer of a wife being drowned in the sea as part of the "cleansing" process.

And another man, this time in Sudan, made sweet love to a goat in 2006. But instead of being punished with prison time, he was told he had to marry the goat. Plus, he had to stick with tradition and give the goat's owner a dowry for his future wife.

Eight
PORN AND SEX TAPES

E ver thought about taping your intimate affairs? Yeah? Oh, that's kinky. No? Well you may be missing out on some of the best publicity you can find. Ask Paris Hilton and Pamela Anderson. From the days of Rob Lowe and Dustin "Screech" Diamond when sex tapes were "oops," to Pamela Anderson and Paris Hilton, whose sex tapes were seductive, to politicians such as Chua Soi Lek, Malaysia's health minister, and John Edwards when sex tapes have been destructive, these private, voyeuristic and erotic home movies have been front-page news since the invention of the motion picture camera. Now with porn becoming more available, and when anyone with a camera can be a porn star, sex tapes are becoming less taboo and can even make a positive mark on someone's career . . . if that's the kind of career they want. Just ask Kim Kardashian and Montana Fishburne.

Porn's been around for a long time. People have always wanted (and will always want) to watch naked people doing the nasty—and have always paid big bucks to see it on film. But when the home video camera came along in the 1970s, you could suddenly film whatever you wanted inside your own home: kids playing in the backyard with the Slip-N-Slide on Christmas morning or a POV of Mom on Dad's stiffy. With today's rapidly advancing technology, the tiniest cameras can catch a huge amount of what's going on. And then with a couple clicks of your mouse, you can upload your magical moving picture for all the world to see.

If you want the thrill of a camera without the Internet fame, ex–porn star Candida Royalle has a solution. She wrote a book called *How to Tell a Naked Man What to Do*, and she suggested hooking up a camera right to the TV. The thing is, don't hit the record button, but just check yourselves out. Or even better, do as Ariel Towne, the Feng Shui Guy, suggests: "You don't have to make a tape. You can just enjoy the moment, be very Zen about it, [watch yourselves in a mirror] and make that moment evaporate. Then create another moment. And it won't end up on the Internet." Of course, there are plenty of people who don't know they're being filmed so they can't weigh in on how they'd like to be (not) recorded. But whether it's a porn star or a sex tape celebrity, the public is almost always fascinated by them and wanting to see more. Porn has been part of our lives, whether we like it or not, ever since humans realized that they get aroused.

I'm kind of upset that I don't. You know why? 'Cause I'm really good.
—JENNY MCCARTHY
TO *ACCESS HOLLYWOOD* ON WHY
SHE WISHES SHE HAD A SEX TAPE

The Business of Sex Tapes

Kevin "KB" Blatt, famous for brokering the Paris Hilton sex tape, has since been crowned *the* celebrity sex tape broker. When he first started, there was no business model. Blatt recounts how he fell into this line of work in 2003, when Rick Salomon's roommate told him he had a tape of Salomon and Paris Hilton servicing each other in night vision. He made a deal with him—$50,000 up front and a back-end deal of one-third of the profits. Blatt then fueled the hype for the tape. "I sent clips of that green-fused X-ray vision tape to *Us Weekly* and *Entertainment Tonight*. It was kind of like the shot heard around the world." Blatt admits he got sued for millions by Salomon, the Hiltons and others since he hadn't obtained all the releases necessary to legally publicize the tape. Blatt also admits that Hilton was an innocent victim at that point, that she hadn't made the tape with the purpose of leaking it. But soon enough, everyone realized they could benefit. *1 Night in Paris* came out legally via Red Light District pictures. Hilton and Salomon signed off on the releases and both are making a pretty penny on it to this day.

Since then, sex tapes involving Tom Sizemore, Dustin Diamond, Chelsea Handler (never released) and plenty of others have all come Blatt's way. "It's become a viable and bankable way to help people become relevant again," explains Blatt. "'D-lebrities' who are broke and bankrupt come to me looking for a last chance to get more work, and to be exposed. Anytime a celebrity sex tape comes out, it's fodder for the tabloids. It becomes the biggest story in the world for at least two days. It doesn't matter who the celebrity is."

It's easy for Blatt to get his hands on sex tapes involving all levels of celebrity, since he receives five to six tapes a month. But what's important to Blatt is differentiating between who's got the most celeb cache. The market—male horn dogs—calls for female celebrities. Male sex tapes don't do as well simply because women don't really want to cough up the money to view a sex tape. "That's why Colin Farrell's sex tape probably wouldn't have sold that well . . . It's the best sex tape that I've ever seen." Blatt also goes on to explain that women who do view sex tapes look for things that are very different from what men are searching for. For example, women were interested in what boots Paris was wearing in her tape (apparently the store that sold the boots that she wore in her sex tape sold out within a week after its release), and in "technique," like to see if they stack up to a Kim Kardashian blow job.

The sex tape list keeps growing, and it's becoming an international sensation. Adult Video News (AVN) even considers sex tapes in their awards shows.

The Internet's Biggest
Purveyor of Kink: Porn

Before leaping into the modern world of sex tapes, let's take a quick look at its inspiration: porn. It's been demonized for the degradation of women, the spread of STDs and the downfall of marriages. But no matter what, porn has its place in US society under the First Amendment. And, with the advent of the Internet, porn has exploded.

This $57 billon global business ($10 billion in the United States alone) has more than 420 million porn pages and 4.2 million websites according to CNN. Forty million Americans regularly visit these sites. The breakdown is 72 percent male versus 28 percent female, and there are consistent reports of porn becoming more and more appealing to women (who are also becoming more involved as directors and producers, not just as stars). You can even get porn on a USB stick, called a Flesh Drive. It's hardly surprising that many people—both men and women—are dealing with a porn addiction. A 2003 study by the Matrimonial Lawyers Association showed that about 56 percent of divorces stemmed from a partner's "obsessive interest" in porn websites.

As porn star and Playboy Radio host Christy Canyon explains, "Porn is definitely pushing the limits. In the 90s . . . they could have a girl giving a guy head and it would make a fortune. Suddenly the new millennium came around and they have to find different outlets, different groups to tap into." Which means finding the newest kinks or fetishes out there and focusing on them in their films. In 1994, a study was conducted by Carnegie Mellon where they found that 48 percent of Internet downloads were not typical pornography, but rather crude and illegal content like bestiality and pedophilia. As soon as people were given the privacy to search for what they wanted, they veered away from traditional sex.

Adam Grayson, founder of SearchExtreme.com (a website where you can pick your fetish and find the porn film that applies) and director of web operations at Evil Angel Productions, goes further. "I don't think this fetish/kink thing really existed before the Internet," he says. He goes on to explain that if someone had a specific fetish in the nineties, they'd have a hard time finding a film that dealt with it. But with the explosion of the Internet, anything could be found, and porn films keep having to fill the voids in content, to focus on every niche fetish out there. "As a porn director friend of mine might say," says Grayson, "when you're producing something, you've got to get that feeling in a guy's gut, which is something that's hard to replicate. The more specific you get, the more you're going to hit guys in that place."

A Quick History of Porn

Porn has been around since humans realized they were turned on by one another. The word "pornography" came from Greeks "writing about prostitutes," with *porne* meaning a harlot. *Science* magazine claims the first pornographic image was created in 33,000 BC, where a figurine was found in a cave outside Stuttgart, Germany. But this wasn't just any figurine; this "Venus" figure was a piece of ivory, carved with huge breasts and vulva. The exaggerated features made it pornographic although there are archeologists who argue these were fertility symbols. In a pit in Leipzig, Germany, the "Adonis from Chernitz" was discovered, made of several clay fragments from the Stone Age that make up what looks to be two people. Archaeologist Harald Staeuble says in the journal *Germania*, "There is strong evidence that this is a copulation scene."

In 2500 BC, Egyptian art was full of life, but it was also full of erections. In hieroglyphs, plenty of naked female dancers would spin around, holding a huge erect penis as a way of worshipping the god Osiris. Some believe this was a fertility ritual; others believe it is one of the first examples of porn. From 1292 to 1075 BC, the Egyptian Turin Erotic Papyrus is thought to have been the first pornographic magazine for men. It had twelve vignettes of artwork dedicated to sex. And there have been plenty of naked, sensual stone sculptures, cave paintings and etchings depicting sex—and we're talking threesomes, oral sex and homosexuality—relics, found in all parts of the world, from Greece to India. Ancient Peru had plenty of ceramic pottery that was decorated with sex scenes by their Moche people. Erotic woodblock prints were popular among the Japanese aristocratic layer of society. In the sixteenth century, Rome became the hub for modern porn, with artists such as the writer Pietro Aretino producing sexually explicit material.

Erotic literature and paintings soon came about and quickly became popular. But almost as quickly, these works of art were banned, and famous writers such as Henry Miller, Gustave Flaubert, Vladimir Nabokov, Anaïs Nin and Emile Zola produced works that caused controversy and sometimes criticism for their highly sexual content. The 1748 *Fanny Hill: Or Memoirs of a Woman of Pleasure* by John Cleland is regarded as the first modern English "erotic novel" to some, with the book touching on floggings and sadomasochism.

Soon enough, porn became even more visual. The daguerreotype camera was invented in the 1830s, and the first photo of a naked woman was sold shortly thereafter. The movie projector was invented in 1890 by Louis Lumière, and the porn business flashed onto the scene, with Eugene Pirou making one of the first skin flicks, *Bedtime for the Bride* (or *Le Coucher de la Marie*, 1896), complete with the actress performing a striptease. And it didn't take long for cinema to get really dirty and kinky, when the Germans made a film with a woman taking it up the butt in the movie named *Am Abend* (1910).

Erotic magazines started to be published once people invented a way to reproduce photographs at a reasonable cost in the late 1800s. The magazines had to be disguised as art publications, but their

Braille Porn

The blind have been given access to porn. Lisa Murphy decided to create her own porno for the blind called *Tactile Mind*. The book is composed of raised images so that the visually impaired consumer can feel out the naked bodies and descriptions, making the photographs come to life.

naked photos were quite shocking—and intriguing—for the times. The Tijuana bibles were underground comic books that were available during the Great Depression and considered by some to be the first porn. When the Polaroid Land camera came out in 1948, it was put to good use for erotic photography. And in 1953, Hugh Hefner's *Playboy* magazine opened its pages to X-rated material in general. The late Bob Guccione's *Penthouse* also added innovation to the X-rated scene in 1965, by being the first magazine to show pubic hair. And in 1970, the advent of the home video camera gave every person wielding one the ability to become amateur pornographers. 1975 led to VHS tapes (so you didn't have to go out to the theaters anymore, hiding under a scarf and hat), and since DVDs, DVR, Blu-ray, high-def and the Internet, no one has had to leave their home to get top-notch porn on their private TVs, computers and smartphones.

First Porn Films

Pornography didn't just start with funny monikers and terrible lounge music. There was a gradual testing of the community standard's waters. The first kiss on film was in the movie aptly named *The Kiss* in 1896, and it caused an uproar in the Catholic Church. Kinetoscopes during that same time showed peep shows of women undressing. *A L'Ecu d'Or ou la bonne auberge* was a French porn film made in 1908 and, according to Patrick Robertson's *Film Facts*, "the earliest pornographic motion picture which can definitely be dated." Argentina's *El Sartorio* was made between 1907 and 1912, with a lot of oral sex. The United States produced its first porn flick called *A Free Ride* (or *A Ride in the Grass*) sometime between 1915 and 1919. And Audrey Munson was the first leading lady in a film to take it all off (but no, she didn't have sex), in the film *Inspiration* (1915).

Porn films were labeled different things during different times. Initially they were called "stags" (because they were often shown at all-men parties, or stag parties) or "blue movies" or "smokers" because of lots of tense men getting their frustrations out on their cigars while watching all that skin on film . . . or "beavers" with women stripping for full-frontal nudity. The 1940s brought about the burlesque short films. Famous model Bettie Page was hot in 1955 in *Teaserama*, and soon "nudie cuties" were popping up in car garages and locker rooms everywhere. *The Immoral Mr. Teas* (1959) by Russ Meyer was considered the first porn feature film, about a man having to get over his fantasies of naked women. The famous director Francis Ford Coppola even made the 1961 *Tonight For Sure!* nudie-cutie flick—where explicit nudity, and not sex, was the focus—before he became legendary with the likes of *The Godfather* and *Apocalypse Now.*

Reuben Sturman is considered the godfather of the American porn industry. He imported Lasse Braun's Swedish porn films, and figured out a way to have porn flicks available to the mainstream. He also invented the peep show.

The first porn film that was a massive hit and coined "porn chic" was the 1972 film *Deep Throat.* It was made for less than $100,000 and has since grossed $600 million worldwide. Its popularity paved the way for porn to become more mainstream. The premise of the film was that the lead character, played by Linda

Lovelace, had her clitoris near the back of her throat—and therefore had an incredible talent for giving blow jobs. But a lot of controversy surrounded the film in the years to come, and there's even a play in theaters called *The Deep Throat Sex Scandal.*

There are the iconic porn films such as *Devil in Miss Jones, Behind the Green Door* and *Debbie Does Dallas.* And now there is a mass production of films filling every sort of fetish and kink out there. Today, you have major porn distribution companies handling the business. Some of the top US porn distributors today are Wicked, Vivid Entertainment, Digital Playground, Adam & Eve and Evil Angel. And there are plenty of mainstream films that

Different Strokes with Older Folks . . .

Time magazine had a 2008 article about what's hot in Japan, and it turns out it's "elder porn." The article's focus was on porn star Shigeo Tokuda, in his seventies, who's cranked out 350 films, such as *Prohibited Nursing* and *Maniac Training of Lolitas,* in more than fourteen years. (He uses a stage name, and it was only after a while that his own wife and daughter discovered what he was doing.)

England also has Grandma Libby Ellis, who is a seventy-year-old erotic model, porn star and escort. And in 2010, Howard Stern interviewed America's Granny Anni May, a seventy-six-year-old porn star who has dabbled in bestiality, anal sex and orgies. She can be found on the website ExploitedMoms.com, where, let's just say, the grandmothers aren't baking or playing bridge.

have bordered on porn. Think Vincent Gallo's *Brown Bunny* (where Chloë Sevigny gives him full-on oral), *Last Tango in Paris* (a lot of buttering up), *9½ Weeks* (Kim Basinger and Mickey Rourke's food scene), *Shortbus* (an autofellatio scene as an opener) and *9 Songs* (one of the UK's most sexually explicit films ever made). These are all films that are acceptable to watch and discuss, even though the steamy sex scenes rival what some porn companies put out.

And porn is keeping up with the future. Three-D is the new dimension for mainstream film, and that includes porn as well. Hong Kong director Christopher Sun budgeted $3.2 million on a sex film called *3D Sex and Zen: Extreme Ecstasy*, and Italy is in the 3-D running as well, with director Tinto Brass getting prepped to do a remake of his sexy version of *Caligula*. *Hustler* is in the works, making a spoof of the 3-D film *Avatar*.

Erotic Magazines

Countless magazines have sprung up since the early days of *Playboy* and *Penthouse*, with publishers knowing they could make tons of money with naked women in their pages. But soon enough, they had to become more inventive, and specialize in different areas to attract different audiences. This includes some magazines coming out with kinky and fetish themes in order to appeal to every type of reader. Just as printed editions of newspapers and magazines have taken a huge hit with the advent of the Internet, so too have porn rags.

Let's look at two magazines, *Playboy* and *Hustler*, that have made an imprint on our culture and have managed to survive.

PLAYBOY

That bunny image has made an indelible mark on society. In 1952, *Playboy* hit the stands with Marilyn Monroe on the cover. The creator, Hugh Hefner, didn't even put a date on the magazine since he was so worried it would bomb. The magazine did explode—but in the best possible way. He sold 50,000 of the first issue. At the end of the 1950s, he sold a million a month. He has made millions from the magazine and built an empire.

But the success of *Playboy* isn't just attributed to the naked women between its covers. As Farrell Hirsch, head of Playboy Radio, explains, *Playboy* has "never been a nudie magazine. The cliché 'I only read it for the articles' wouldn't make sense with something like *Penthouse* or *Hustler*. *Playboy* magazine launched the careers of Ray Bradbury and Stephen King. The autobiography of Malcolm X started as an essay in *Playboy* magazine. It's one of the most important pieces of literature of the twentieth century. *Playboy* has been a real fighter in the liberties of minorities and women, and at the same time, *Playboy* has been a great supporter of the American military over the years." When asked the inevitable, if the magazine could be viewed as degrading to women, Hirsch explains, "Some say *Playboy* has objectified women; some say it's empowered women, saying you're free to sleep with or be whoever you'd like. You should explore your freedom and do what you want. No one is coerced into being in the magazine or hanging at the mansion."

Playboy is the most famous adult magazine in the world. Published in more than twenty-five countries, the *Playboy* empire has a web, TV and radio presence. The various radio programs, with porn stars and playmates hosting segments, are all sexual in nature. The hosts are usually eager to do outrageous, kinky things on air, such as getting whipped till they bleed, leading around a human pony and taking on a sex-toy machine. Of course, it's a wild ride in the sound booth, with no shortage of shock factor. Hirsch explains, "For us, the kinkier, the better. We just keep pushing to obscene levels."

All of these enterprises have continued successfully in large part due to the fact that the Playboy Bunny symbol and Hugh Hefner are iconic fixtures in cultures worldwide. Hirsch praises Hefner and his life's work. "He has a huge scope. So the company does as well . . . All great works of art are the product of one driving force . . . That's what Hefner has done with his company. It takes a visionary to make something great." And he's not the only one who agrees with this statement. A documentary was made on Hefner in 2010, called *Hugh Hefner: Playboy, Activist and Rebel*, which focuses on Hefner's life and accomplishments.

HUSTLER

Hustler magazine is another example of sustained success in the world of adult entertainment. Its creator, Larry Flynt, is a historical fixture in pop culture and politics. In 1974, the first issue of

Hustler magazine hit the shelves. However, Flynt was already making a name for himself as a troublemaker and protector of free speech rights. He was sent to jail for his "crimes," and shot and paralyzed outside a courthouse by a man angry because Flynt had published interracial material.

"My goal has always been to expand the perimeters of free speech," says Flynt in an interview. "Some people realize the contribution I made to free expression or human sexuality. There are other detractors [who think] I'm just this seedy old man in the basement of this building cranking out pornography every day. There are two schools of thought on that and I leave my own detractors to their own misery." He goes on to explain that the cause is especially important to him since he was shot and paralyzed

The Crossover

Porn is like the kinky industry, setting and exhibiting the best and worst of trends. But some people enter porn for the wrong reasons, thinking they'll become "respectable" household names. As porn star and Playboy Radio host Christy Canyon explains, "You go into (porn) because you love sex. Not because you want to cross into the mainstream . . . You're not going to cross over . . ." But actually, a couple have done so. For example, Kung Fu superstar Jackie Chan starred in the porn flick *All in the Family* in 1975. And *Rocky's* Sylvester Stallone starred in the porn flick *Party at Kitty and Stud's*, playing "Stud" for $200 before he became a household name.

thirty years ago, and that maybe if he hadn't been shot, he might feel differently. But still he says, "I think people need to be free. People need to be free to make their own decisions."

Today, *Hustler* is an empire. Theresa Flynt, Larry Flynt's daughter, helped put the Hustler Hollywood stores on the map, and she talks about what she is most proud of when it comes to the company as a whole. "It's how we've become a global brand," she says. "In the '60s, we were strip bars and go-go clubs. In the '70s and '80s, we were a magazine and magazine distribution company. And in the '90s, we expanded onto the Internet, we opened a casino, we launched retail stores, and manufactured a clothing line. Additionally, we're the largest provider of adult content on broadcast television. And there's much more on the horizon."

Today's Porn: Sex Tapes

Terrible acting, cheesy music and a prison guard who gets laid by four scantily clad and sexy female inmates can mean only one thing: old-school porn. Today's porn is different and there's a new branch to the evolving smut tree. Sex tapes are the new YouTube of pornography. Anyone can make one and, if they're brave enough, they can even post them onto the Internet where anyone can see, vote or virally pass it along to friends. Throw a celebrity into the mix and you've got tabloid news fodder that will push wars, genocide and the cure for cancer onto page two.

Marilyn Monroe is the biggest sex icon of all time. So if an X-rated home movie of Monroe surfaced, it would be the biggest sex tape of all time, right? Now it appears that there might be one, but it doesn't sound like anyone will see it anytime soon. A New York businessman who bought it for $1.5 million (from the son of a dead FBI informant) plans to stow it away for good. "Not going to make a Paris Hilton out of her," he supposedly said, according to Keya Morgan, a collector who brokered the deal. The apparent sneak peeks at the silent, black-and-white, fifteen-minute, 16-millimeter film made sometime in the 1940s or '50s reveal Monroe on her knees, giving oral sex to who some people think might be a Kennedy. Then again, others claim this sex tape is a hoax.

Celebrity sex tape broker Kevin Blatt considers the first celebrity sex tape to be in the form of photos, specifically of Jackie Onassis. *Playmen* magazine (Italy's version of *Playboy*) obtained nude photos of her skinny-dipping in 1971 and published them. In America, *Hustler* magazine followed suit and published them in 1975. "It wasn't a tape but it was the first celebrity to be exposed in a way that the general public took such an interest in it," says Blatt.

Jayne Kennedy was a famous African American woman who became one of the first female sportscasters in the 1970s. She also became the first African American woman to be on the cover of *Playboy*. And she also had a homemade sex tape floating around. Circulation was limited in the '80s—no Internet—so it didn't damage her career as much as it could have. However, it was famous for a kinky little maneuver some like to call "fisting." Use your imagination.

Vivid Entertainment claims it has a Jimi Hendrix sex tape, of the legendary musician doing it with two women while his 'fro is tied up in a bandanna. Apparently, there isn't any audio of this tape done more than forty years ago, and there are those who speculate that it may be manipulated and not a real tape at all.

In 1988, actor Rob Lowe caught a lot of heat—and not just in the bedroom. He made a couple of sex tapes and it garnered quite a bit of bad press. No one close to him was especially surprised since the actor was known for his healthy libido, cocksmanship and fondness for filming his sexual exploits. But it didn't help when it was revealed that one of his bedroom ladies was only sixteen years old (he was twenty-four). He later went into rehab for sex addiction.

In 1998, Pamela Anderson and her then-husband, Tommy Lee, gave us a boatload of sex on their honeymoon in what is considered to be officially the first real celebrity sex tape. They got millions from the distribution company Internet Entertainment Group. When the videotape version came out, it was the bestselling porn tape in history, and was ranked nineteen out of 100 top adult films in 2009.

This tape would actually prove to be a follow-up performance for Anderson, who had already made one with Poison's lead singer, Bret Michaels. Yet that tape surfaced years after the act was done.

In 1993, the lead singer of Mötley Crüe, Vince Neil, filmed himself having a threesome with porn star Janine Lindemulder and model Brandy Ledford. In 1998, the tape was released. Ledford wasn't happy about it so her face is blurred in the tape.

He did it all for the nookie? In 2005, Fred Durst, rock-n-roller turned director, made a little movie on his cell phone. The raw video of him having sex with a model was leaked online, and Durst then sued several websites for $70 million for publicizing it.

He later dropped the suit, and many wonder if he hadn't leaked it himself.

In 2006, "Screech," the character that made Dustin Diamond famous on the TV show *Saved by the Bell*, pretended to be shocked when a sex tape came out showing him fooling around with two women in a bathtub. The truth soon came out that he knew exactly what was going on, and had hoped the tape would help bring him back some fame. He can be found at porn conventions today, promoting the tape.

Actor Colin Farrell was not too happy when a 2004 tape of him bunny-hopping on *Playboy* model Nicole Narain was viewed by the world. He sued to have the tape blocked but it was still leaked by ICG (Internet Commerce Group). Today, at least part of it can be seen at the Museum of Sex in New York.

Joanie "Chyna" Laurer showed off more than her wrestling skills in 2004 by making a sex tape with ex-boyfriend/wrestler Sean Waltman (aka X-Pac). She decided to call it *1 Night in China*, an homage to Paris Hilton's tape. Don't ever say Paris Hilton didn't have an influence on other artists.

Jenna Lewis was famous for being a *Survivor* contestant. But she didn't survive the embarrassment of everyone finding out that she secretly owned the adult website that featured a "leaked" sex tape of her and her ex-husband. She was raking in the profits all the while protesting the tape's release.

Tom Sizemore, perhaps known more for his connection to former DC madam Heidi Fleiss than his acting, has a condition some men pay lots of money to obtain: a long-lasting erection. Sizemore's stiffy can last for hours, and the condition is called a priapism, "an abnormal, persistent, and painful erection that won't go down in spite of orgasm," according to doctors. So he decided to take full advantage of it and made a sex tape in 2005. He filmed himself having sex with prostitutes for eight hours straight.

R. Kelly was accused of having sex with a minor, a thirteen-year-old girl, and urinating on her. It was caught on tape. At first he received twenty-one counts of kiddy porn. But it was reduced to seventeen because you couldn't actually see intercourse on the tape. Another girlfriend claimed he walked around with a duffel bag full of homemade sex tapes. But despite it all, he was acquitted.

The Rolling Stones' Mick Jagger's daughter Elizabeth, who is a model, was caught on tape doing it with her boyfriend, Calum Best, in a nightclub. A British judge banned the video from being broadcast.

Notorious Olympic ice-skater Tonya Harding, who hired a goon to break her rival Nancy Kerrigan's knee in 1994, decided to take her notoriety to a deeper infamy. Later that same year, she made a sex tape with her ex-husband, Jeff Gillooly, called *Wedding Night* (*Penthouse* published it in 1994).

Plenty of moms have sacrificed their dignity in order to make ends meet for their children. But "Octomom" (aka Nadya Suleman) put herself and her children in a precarious position when she over-procreated. In 2011, in order to pay for diapers, she starred in a fetish video where she whipped a man who pretended to have an infantilism fetish. Decked out in a diaper and bonnet, the man—a radio DJ who did it as a joke and to potentially make some cash—curled over her lap as she lashed him for being a bad boy.

South Korea's famous singer Baek Ji-Young watched her career shit the bed in 2001 when a sex tape of her was broadcast on a pay-per-view channel in her country. She was doing it with her manager, who supposedly leaked the tape.

Careful about whose sex tape you're selling. Latin sensation Jennifer Lopez sued her ex-husband Ojani Noa when he tried to get some hard cash for their honeymoon sex tapes.

Verne Troyer (aka Mini-Me of the Austin Powers flicks) didn't appreciate a sex tape of him and his twenty-two-year-old ex-girlfriend and aspiring model being leaked. He sued the distributor and managed to keep parts of it from airing.

Actor Kelsey Grammer may have gotten ahead of himself when he sued Internet Entertainment Group for obtaining his homemade sex tape, which was stolen from his private collection. He had hired private investigators to find the tape and they determined it was IEG. Thing is, IEG didn't have the tape and hadn't even heard of it (till then!). Grammer quickly dropped the suit.

Reality star Kim Kardashian made a sex tape in 2007 with her ex-boyfriend R&B singer Ray J. Although she claims that the release of the sex tape was "humiliating," it did elevate her reality star power, put her on the cover of *Playboy*, create a brand name for herself and continues to keep her and her family in gossip magazines.

Actor Laurence Fishburne's daughter, Montana, decided to find fame by going straight to the porn company Vivid Entertainment and negotiating rights to her sex tape. TMZ quotes her as saying: "I've watched how successful Kim Kardashian became and I think a lot of it was due to the release of her sex tape by Vivid. I'm hoping the same magic will work for me."

The Real Housewives have taken reality TV shows by storm, throwing the image of the typical housewife waiting at home with an apron and cooking meals to the wayside. One housewife of New Jersey, Danielle Staub, decided to take reality programming to a new low when she recorded a seventy-five-minute sex tape with an unknown man. *Hustler* now distributes the tape of this fifty-year-old mother of two.

Long Island Lolita Amy Fisher built on her infamy when she decided to make a sex tape with her husband and sell it to a porn company. The once-scorned lover who shot her boyfriend Joey Buttafuoco's wife in the face and served jail time for it has declared herself bisexual and has her own porn site.

Fisher wasn't the only one who benefited from this twisted love triangle. After Buttafuoco got out of jail for raping Fisher, he made his own sex tape with his third wife at a party at the home of an adult film executive. Staying classy.

American Idol finalist Jessica Sierra signed on to play herself in her raunchy sex tape called *Jessica Sierra Superstar.* The distributor, again Vivid Entertainment, released a statement saying, "Jessica clearly has more talent than just singing."

Forget the economic crisis. Greeks found something a little more intriguing to focus on in 2010: a sex tape made by Greek pop star Julia Alexandratou, apparently together with a French porn star in a whirlpool bath and lounging with Dom Pérignon. Supposedly, it's the first sex tape made by a Greek celebrity. Proud Grecians decided to spend their money on the DVD, and a quarter of a million copies were sold within the first ten days of its release. Easter candles were even made to Alexandratou's "likeness" and sold like spanakopitas.

India flipped out when their holy man, Nithyananda Swami, who had millions of followers in Southern India, was arrested for obscenity, putting a dent on his holier-than-thou image. His religious mission even has offices in various countries like the United States. But that all changed when a sex tape emerged of him with two women. He claims the video's fake, but he still stepped down and out of the spiritual spotlight.

In 2008, Max Mosley, the British president of the International Automobile Federation, got caught on camera in an S&M orgy role-play as a Nazi officer in a concentration camp. Prostitutes were dressed as prisoners and guards, and even administered lice inspections to keep it realistic. All of it was caught on film by a prostitute who snuck a camera into her bra and recorded the event. This from a guy whose father was Sir Oswald Mosley, an old buddy of Hitler's.

Former Miss California Carrie Prejean may be religiously conservative, but she isn't that conservative sexually, or in front of cameras. At age seventeen, she performed solo on camera for an ex-boyfriend. She lost her beauty crown due to the video and for statements she made against gay marriage. When she decided to sue the pageant for discrimination and slander, they shot right back, saying she still owed them more than $5,000 for the boob job they helped her get.

KISS's Gene Simmons was caught in a black-and-white video in 2008 of him having his way with a model. It's rumored Simmons has slept with more than 4,600 women. In the tape, he has his shirt on, his pants wrapped around his ankles and his shoes still on.

There are plenty of pro soccer players who have been caught on tape. For example, three UK soccer players, Frank Lampard, Kieron Dyer and Rio Ferdinand, were all kicking up bedsheets in a group sex tape.

Another intriguing example is former Manchester United player Dwight Yorke, who along with his fellow soccer player Mark Bosnich was filmed with a few women in a "cross-dressing" orgy.

After Indonesia's pop star Ariel (or Nazril Irham) was accused of distributing sex tapes, he became the first celebrity to suffer the consequences of Indonesia's strict pornography law (which started in 2008) and was sentenced to prison in 2011. He was featured in three sex tapes, and he was accused of distributing other sex tapes featuring other celebrities.

The Politics of Sex Tapes

There are three easy ways to lose an election or get impeached from office. The first is hiring illegal immigrants as you campaign against them. The second is screaming like a banshee and losing it on stage after a primary loss. The third is showing up on a sex tape, especially if it's with someone other than your spouse. Men and women of public service have long been the victim of ego, power and its subsequent influence on their own fidelity. But what separates one from the other are the foolish politicians who decide that it's a good idea to bang the campaign manager while the film is rolling.

During his presidential run, Senator John Edwards decided it'd be fun to let his documentary filmmaker/lover Rielle Hunter tape him having sex with her. The tape was produced around the time Hunter was four or five months pregnant with their love child, with Edwards going down on her and even clowning around for the camera. Hunter left the tape in a box where Edwards's former aide, Andrew Young, claimed to have found it and then brought it to the attention of authorities.

Former Taipei City councilwoman Chu Mei-feng was forced to resign because she was secretly filmed having sex with her married lover in 2001. Police found cameras all over her office, home and car. The lingerie she wore on the sex tape sold out in many stores. She also managed to turn things around in her favor by becoming a singer.

Less kink, more fink. Atlantic City councilman Eugene Robinson, a Baptist minister, found himself in a motel having sex with a prostitute in 2006. Unbeknownst to him, he was being secretly filmed by his rival. A secret camera had been installed in the room and the prostitute was a frame job. Former City Council president Craig Callaway tried to get Robinson to resign by blackmailing him with the tape; however, Robinson went to the police instead. Callaway was sent to jail for his actions. Robinson went on to say that he had consensual sex with the woman and if there was any money exchanged, it was so that she could buy some soda.

Malaysia's health minister, Chua Soi Lek, a married father of three, at first refused to resign in 2008 when a sex tape was leaked of him with a woman in a hotel room. He finally did resign, and apologized with his wife by his side.

Indonesians didn't appreciate one of their senior politicians and parliamentary secretary of Golkar, Yahya Zaini, being part of a sex tape with singer Maria Eva that spread online in 2006. Zaini resigned quickly thereafter, and Eva went on record to say she had been in love with him despite Zaini being married.

India's eighty-six-year-old politican Narayan Dutt Tiwari was forced to resign in 2009 when a tape surfaced of him with three women in bed. Gotta give the man high marks for his trifecta stamina considering his age!

Italy's prime minister, Silvio Berlusconi, has made quite a reputation for himself. And even though there's no video evidence (yet) of his sexual dalliances, there is an audio tape of him making out with a call girl, where he encourages her to masturbate.

Another sex tale that doesn't need video proof but was audio-recorded was of California State assemblyman Mike Duvall, who likes to call himself a "family values warrior." He forgot he was still miked when he revealed to a friend that he was really getting into spanking his lover.

Sex Rehab

One popular recurring trend among famous cheaters are celebrities going into sex rehab as soon as they're caught cheating. Whether or not it's sincere, it's hard not to think it's an easy way out for some of these dogs.

Actor David Duchovny, who plays a sex-obsessed writer on the TV show *Californication*, went into sex rehab while married to Téa Leoni. Life is sometimes just as strange as fiction.

English comedian and cocksmith Russell Brand admitted he once checked himself into rehab for sex addiction. He's now married to singer (and latex queen) Katy Perry.

Beatty's Seduction

A book came out on actor Warren Beatty called *Star: How Warren Beatty Seduced America*. A stud in his day, he was someone who probably would have qualified for sex-addiction therapy. He has supposedly had more than 12,000 sex partners!

Golfer Tiger Woods was the classic image of a clean-cut sportsman who had it all: career, money and family. But with one swing of Elin Nordegren's golf club against his SUV, Tiger's world was turned upside down.

Tiger blew it all by not only having affairs, but having affairs with women who were more than willing to come forward and speak about Woods's questionable sex behaviors. Coughing up big bucks to hang out with hookers and mix it up with threesomes, Tiger garnered a reputation from the girls as a talented and insatiable lover.

Of course all good things must come to an abrupt and train-wreck end, so Woods entered sex rehab so that his wife and all the world could see he was healing. His marriage inevitably fizzled into a divorce. Some sponsors pulled their endorsement deals with him. And he fell from the ranking as the world's number one golfer.

Nine

KINK LINGO

E very community has its own lingo. In the sex world, that
language can be vast. Here are some words that might be
worth knowing the next time you decide to show up at an
S&M club or tune in online to a kinky social networking site, or
you just want to impress your lover:

A Big Night with Rose Palms or Arm-Wrestling the Purple-Headed
Monster or Flogging the Dolphin: This refers to a male masturbating.

A Night in with the Girls: This refers to a female masturbating.

Abe Lincoln: The guy comes all over his partner's shaved-off pubic area and then puts the semen around the area to create a beard.

Alligator Fuckhouse: When a man bites a woman's neck, locks his arms with hers and rolls around, with his penis still inside the whole time.

Anasyrma: Skirts with no panties underneath.

Angry Dragon: After coming in someone's mouth, smack the back of their head so they snort it out of their nose.

ATM: Ass to mouth. See also *Hydralingus*.

Barry Manilow's Saggy Crown Jewels: Refers to an elderly man's testicles.

Bear: This is a large gay man, who usually likes to smoke cigars and is infatuated with bears.

Bernard Manning's Morning Toast: Usually done in cheap porn flicks, a male ejaculates on a cracker, which is then ingested by another person.

Bi-Kinky: A person in the BDSM scene who's heterosexual but will "play" with same-sex people.

Bi-Possible: A heterosexual who is willing to have bisexual sex.

Bigs: Another word for "grown-ups," or those who take care of people who like to pretend they are much younger than they are. See also *Littles*.

Black Party: Specific to the gay leather world, only those wearing black can attend these parties.

Blood Sports: Intense SM play, with cutting, piercing and anything else that can cause blood to flow.

The Blumpkin: The act of getting a blow job while defecating.

Body Modification: Tattooing, branding, cutting or anything else that will change the body's appearance in fairly primitive ways.

Body Service: When a submissive takes care of a Dominant's needs, from bathing to grooming.

Body Worship: When a submissive gives oral contact to any part of the Dominant's body. .

Boot Boy: A (usually gay) submissive with a fetish for boots and who will give them oral service.

Bootlicking: When a submissive cleans his Dominant's boots with his tongue and other cleaning products as a show of respect.

Booty Call: When someone contacts a partner after midnight to come over for no-strings-attached intercourse.

Boston City Roll: When a male performer curls up, puts his penis in his mouth and rolls down a hill, with the goal of crashing into nude women. Only porn legend Ron Jeremy is thought to have ever pulled this off.

Boston Pancake: A guy craps on his lover's chest, pats it down with his butt and then ejaculates, giving it the appearance of a pancake with syrup.

Boy: A male submissive, usually in the gay world.

Breath Control: The Dominant/top is in control of the way the submissive/bottom is breathing—and will block their breath as long as they desire.

Brown Shower: Similar to a golden shower, but urine is replaced with human excrement.

Butch: Usually in lesbian relationships, the Dominant/top is more mannish and "butchy."

Cage: A submissive is sometimes kept in a cage by their Dominant. There's also the "cock cage," where a penis shaft may be locked.

Camel Toe: When vagina lips can be seen through clothing.

Carpet Muncher: Someone who engages in cunnilingus. Usually refers to a lesbian.

Chili Chopper: A painful act when chili powder is sprinkled on a penis.

The Cleveland Steamer: The act of defecating on a sex partner's body.

C2C: Cock to cock. Usually referring to gay sex.

Coney Island Whitefish: A used condom that washed up onshore.

Cream Pie: When a man orgasms without a condom into a woman, and then watches the semen drip out.

Daddy: Someone willing to be a paternal or mentoring figure to a submissive.

Daisy Chain: A group of people performing oral sex on one another in a chain.

Dirty Sanchez: After sex, the guy will take his penis out and then slide it across his lover's upper lip, so that it looks like a (white) "mustache." Sometimes confused for the popular European take on it, the "Hitler," which involves feces. Sometimes can refer to someone sticking his finger into an anus and then making his partner smell it.

Dog in a Bathtub: When a man attempts to place his testicles in an anus.

Doggy Style: When a woman is taken from behind, usually resting on her hands and knees.

Donkey Punch: When a man or woman is engaged in anal sex and, while behind their partner, punches them in the back of the head or neck so that all of the butt muscles contract, making the experience more intense for the partner on top.

DP: Double penetration. Yes, one penis in the vagina, another penis or sex toy in the anus.

Dungeon: A place where S&M occurs, in private or public.

Feeding the Horse: Sometimes, having foreplay with a vagina can look like you're feeding a horse. Yee-haw!

Felching: After anal sex, the man or woman extracts the semen from the rectum with their mouth.

Femme: Another term for "lipstick lesbian," where she takes on a more feminine attitude.

Flag/flagging: Different color-coded bandannas that tell other people what kinky sexual behaviors you're into. An example: flagging to the right or left, you are letting someone know if you're Dominant (left) or submissive (right).

Flying: A sensation past the point of pain, when the person is feeling what's beyond pain.

Froggy Style: When the woman sits on top of the man and moves up and down.

Gender Fuck: This is someone who partly tries to switch genders, mostly for shock value. An example: a woman who uses a strap-on, or a guy who stuffs a bra.

Glass Bottom Boat: A person defecates on a glass coffee table while their partner is looking up at them from underneath.

Hot Lunch: Defecating on a person's mouth covered with cling wrap.

Hydralingus: Another word for ATM.

The Ice Cream Stand: A woman does a headstand; her partner puts ice cream in between her legs and eats it.

Karezza: A technique where a man's penis remains inside a woman only moving to maintain his erection.

Littles (or Ageplayers): Adults who see themselves as little kids and like having "grown-ups" to take care of them who are referred to as "bigs."

Messy: People who like to get wet and messy during sex, whether it's from body fluids or foods.

Motorboating: Stuffing your mouth in a pair of breasts and mimicking the sound of an off-board motor.

MTA: Mouth to ass.

Munch: A way for kinky people to hang with new and old friends in a "vanilla" setting, like a public restaurant.

Nuts and Bolts: Men's genitals.

Pain Slut: A masochist who's really into pain.

Pansexuality: When kinky people from all sexual orientations—heterosexual, homosexual, transgender and so on—hang out together.

Panty Training: Where a Dominant forces a male submissive to wear feminine garb in order to embarrass him. It can also be "petticoat training," where the panties have ruffles on them.

Pearl Necklace: When a man ejaculates on a woman's neck, giving her the appearance of wearing a pearl necklace.

Percussion Play: This involves all forms of hitting, from paddling to spanking to caning to flogging.

Pink Balls: The flip (gender) side of blue balls, this is when a woman experiences sexual frustration.

Ponyboy/Ponygirl: When a submissive/bottom takes on their role in animal play.

Purple Mushroom: While receiving fellatio, the man takes out his penis and smacks the woman's forehead with it, leaving the impression of a mushroom above her brow.

Pushy (or Greedy) Sub: A submissive who pushes the limits and attempts to be as misbehaved as possible in order to receive as much attention as possible from their Dominant.

Reverse Cowgirl: When a woman is on top of the man during sex, but facing his feet as she rides him.

Rusty Trombone: When a person is licked on the anus, and at the same time, the licker reaches around to play with their genitals, similar in appearance to playing a trombone.

Sailor's Cup of Tea: Anal sex.

69: When two people perform oral sex on each other at the same time.

Sharps: Sharp instruments used in S&M, like knives and razors.

Sissy (or Sissy Slut): A submissive male who cross-dresses.

Snowballing: A term for semen swapping that's usually done through kissing after a man ejaculates in a person's mouth.

The Stranger: Masturbating after a male's hand has fallen asleep.

Streaking: The act of running naked in public.

Subspace: The euphoria a submissive experiences from being dominated.

Tea Bag: When a man dips his scrotum into his partner's mouth.

Toilet Slave: A submissive who is attentive to their Dominant's toilet habits, cleaning their toilet and sometimes even acting as one.

Tooth and Fang: Scratching and biting during sex.

Tossing the Salad: Said to have originated in prison, the act of tonguing a person's anus.

Tranny Chaser: Someone who is attracted to transvestites.

Transgendered: Someone drawn to becoming the opposite sex and identifying with that gender.

Transvestite: Someone who dresses like the opposite sex.

Transsexual: Someone who thinks they should actually be the opposite sex, and will often have operations to try to change themselves.

Vanilla: A nonkinky person.

Verbal Abuse: Humiliating and verbally abusing a submissive/bottom in order for the sub/bottom to be fulfilled.

Voyeurism: Taking pleasure in surreptitiously watching someone with or without them knowing, and often during a sexual act.

Water Sports: Anything that includes body waste in an erotic way.

Yiffing: Having sex in the virtual world, whether in video games, social networking or sex chat rooms.

WIITWD ("What It Is That We Do"): It's a nonjudgmental way of looking at the different things people do in kinky sex.

Zepplins: Another way to refer to a very large set of breasts.

ABOUT THE AUTHOR

Eva Christina has written for NBC's *Las Vegas* and *Law & Order: Special Victims Unit*, and is a filmmaker. She was also a senior editor of *Notorious* magazine. She lives in California.